EVIL SPIRITS

UNABRIDGED

BISHOP
DONNELL LONG

Contents

Forward

---※---

Nothing To Joke About

I sincerely tell you that this information has been "nothing to joke about!" It is no laughing matter to be called by God to expose this adversary and set people free from demonic holds. It is a serious business that should not be taken lightly. Keep your heart open to hear the voice of God. Some of what you read here will surprise and shock you. Press on -- the truth will make you free.

This earth we live on has been cursed since the first man and woman walked upon it - almost 6,000 years ago (see Genesis 3:16-19). These curses have been passed down from generation to generation (see Exodus 20:5).

-Apostle, C.L. Long, [1]

---

1. Watch Out For Evil Spirits, 1995 1st Edition

Introduction

What do you think of when you hear *"spiritual warfare"*? Simply put, the ongoing conflict in the unseen (*spiritual*) world ultimately influences what we see and experience physically. Make no mistake -- there is no "neutral ground" in the spirit realm *(Matthew 12:30)*. While God and his heavenly host are standing ready to protect and serve every believer's need, there exist forces hell-bent on killing, stealing, and destroying *(John 10:10)* any person captured by their influence.

For the believer, this is doubly important; the evil forces exposed in this book work tirelessly to prevent or weaken you in your walk with the Lord. *This warfare is the fight for your soul.* The enemy aims to move us far from God and His will for our lives. Be encouraged by knowing that God, indeed, has a plan for your life. I pray that with this book, the word of God, and His guidance, you are put on guard against satan's devices. You'll discover how the devil uses everyday stress, societal oppression, and personal despair as part of his spiritual battle plan.

This conflict is much larger in scale than many Christians like to believe. Many consider spiritual warfare a one-time event (like conversion) or a dramatic response to rare supernatural occurrences. The truth is our spiritual battle wages continually, day by day *(Romans 8:36)*. Thanks be to God who gives us the victory through our Lord and Savior, Jesus Christ; we will indeed emerge more than conquerors.

All Bible-believing, born-again Christians are at risk if we remain ignorant of his schemes *(2 Corinthians 2:11)*. This is spiritual "warfare," after all. No one is exempt: from the pulpit to the parking lot — new believer to the seasoned saint, the enemy in this wise has no *respect* for person or title.

As you grow in your understanding, guard yourself against the error of attributing more power to the devil than he is due. He is a defeated foe! However, like all errors, they occur in a variety of ways: ignorance of scripture, misinformed teachings, unbalanced interest in the enemy, or misplaced zeal can cause a person to be carried away by their ideas and imaginations *(Proverbs 3:5-6, Acts 19:13-15, James 1:14)*. Missteps in this manner are a lot easier to make than one would like to admit. These missteps are the open doors by which the devil gains access to cause harm. We should always focus on Jesus *(Hebrews 12:2)*. Adopting a disciple's heart, we can approach the master and ask Him to "teach us how to pray."

I hope to uncover many misunderstandings as we walk through this study together. One of the reasons many are willing to avoid this subject is its stigmas. For instance, the term *"demon-possessed,"* translated in Matthew 4:24 and Matthew 8:16 (KJV), *more accurately implies oppression*, <u>not</u> possession. Secondly, the term *"possession"* refers to ownership, and if you belong to Christ, any encroachment from the enemy is illegal and must be treated as such. We'll discuss this in depth later, but for the moment, consider the woman in Luke 13:11. The Bible stated that she had a "spirit of infirmity" for eighteen years. When Jesus took notice of her, he identified who she *truly belonged to* by calling her a *"daughter of Abraham"* in Luke 13:16. This account shows two things: the enemy has no rights to your life, and secondly, if anyone deserves deliverance from the enemy's hand, it should be those whom Christ has redeemed (Psalms 107:2, John 8:36).

For the non-believer, however, there are no such guarantees (Isaiah 3:10-11). Those who dismiss God or ignore the reality of evil spirits are blind by pride and carnal reasoning. This "human way" of thinking begins with a superficial use of temporal wisdom and marks the beginning of a steady decline into a downright demonic mindset. Nothing describes this decline as vividly as James 3:15-16:

> *"This wisdom descendeth not from above, but is earthly, sensual, devilish. For where envying and strife is, there is confusion and every evil work."* (James 3:15-16 KJV emphasis added)

God is constantly found in scripture, reminding his people of the importance of staying faithful. As a Pastor, I emphasize that those of us who are believers must remain believers, or we risk falling in the same way, *"denying the Lord that bought us"* (2Peter 2:1) and slipping beyond the point of repentance into a mind that is *"reprobate concerning the faith"* (Romans 1:28-29, 2 Timothy 3:8, 1 Timothy 4:1-4).

I hope to strengthen you with insight that will aid in making you effective in your service to our Lord Jesus. We must do all we can not to become sidetracked or succumb to the devil's pitfalls and his influences. As the church, we are under attack as a whole. Every worker must be equipped for ministry in their respective place. When this happens, God's message can flow unhindered, reaching the lost, making disciples, and freeing those captive.

Chapter 1

Satan & His Devices

"Put on the whole armour of God, that ye may be able to stand against the wiles of the devil." Ephesians 6:11 (KJV)

***

What are "wiles"? The scriptures reveal them simply as the enemy's method to fool, trap, and entice humankind. There is truth to the maxim, "The greatest trick Satan ever accomplished was to make the world believe that he doesn't exist."

Many "believers" are unprepared for what satan uses for schemes and traps; he doesn't fight fair, nor should we expect him to. In this day and time, we must be aware of our surroundings, discerning as we encounter different situations. Without this insight, many fall victim to satan's influence in several ways. Let's discover some of these tricks and schemes by looking closely at the enemy's Nature and Tactics.

He Lies & Is The Father of Lies

"For you are the children of your father the devil, and you love to do the evil things he does. He was a murderer from the beginning and a hater of truth—there is not an iota of truth in him. When he lies, it is perfectly normal; for he is the father of liars." John 8:44 (TLB)

Let the reader be warned: the devil is a liar. Everything he presents or argues is born

Many "believers" are unprepared for what satan uses for schemes and traps; he doesn't fight fair after all.

from an eternally bent nature rooted in falsehood and deceit. Nothing from him or his agents can be trusted, considered helpful, or suitable for any reason, no matter how practical it may seem. Once you understand the nature of a person, place, or thing, it is less likely to take you by surprise.

It was Eve who was first deceived. Never knowing sin, she had no point of reference (besides God's command) to guard herself against the serpent's suggestions. With seemingly virtuous intentions, "to be like God" (Genesis 3:5), Eve took the fruit, perhaps feeling justified by its supposedly practical benefits (Genesis 3:6). As he does with us, the enemy sows seeds of doubt, suggesting that we, like Eve, may not have fully understood what God meant when he spoke from the beginning.

He Blinds The Minds of Unbelievers

"But if our gospel be hid, it is hid to them that are lost: In whom the god of this world hath blinded the minds of them which believe not, lest the light of the glorious gospel of Christ, who is the image of God, should shine unto them. For we preach not ourselves, but Christ Jesus the Lord; and ourselves your servants for Jesus' sake" (2 Corinthians 4:3-5 KJV emphasis added).

This blindness can also be described as ignorance or willful blindness. As we approach the end time, the Bible warns us of several things that will happen in continual succession, both in and around people worldwide.

- Heady and high-minded attitudes (2 Timothy 3:4)

- An increase of knowledge/Access to information (Daniel 12:4-6)

- Overall rejection of absolute truth (Romans 1:28)

Such things make it difficult for people to accept the gospel message in its entirety or at all. Void of God's word leaves us vulnerable to presumption, puffed up in the pride of "stats and facts," leaving us blind to the enemy's true intention, keeping us ignorant through the jargon of "information overload."

He Masquerades In Costumes of Light & Righteousness

2 Corinthians 11:14 (NIV) And no wonder, for Satan himself masquerades as an angel of light.

In the eleventh chapter of 2 Corinthians, Paul zealously pleads with the people of Corinth not to be fooled by religious deception, which aims to masquerade as true faith. *The trick begins by <u>claiming</u> to be the "<u>same as</u>" in name or experience.* The targets of such masquerades are those already saved and those previously presented with the gospel and near to believing in Christ.

This demonic masquerade gains its advantage through its use of subtlety and craftiness. One example would be teachings that proclaim Jesus but don't accept all that Christ teaches. Such deception appeals to one's unrepented desires, suggesting "another way" to look at scripture. The error of this deception is called "compromise." Scriptural compromise is the subtle suggestion that convinces a person that they can keep their sin and "their salvation" too (Titus 1:16).

Bolder masquerades center on spiritual experiences or similarities in acts of worship.

> *Scriptural compromise is the subtle suggestion that convinces a person that they can keep their sin and their Jesus, too.*

I will cover the dangers of occult and pagan traditions later. However, other Christian departures declare to have biblical roots but differ by claiming "divine override." Such claims usually accompany a dream or angelic visitation to authenticate the "new doctrine." These are the sort that claim authority "from their dreams" (Jude 1:8 NLT) and not from God.

Many of the most popular false doctrines of our age claim their legitimacy through angelic visitations; many of these "departures of the faith" even cite the Archangels Gabriel or Micheal by name. "Wonderous signs" are emphasized above the written word to legitimize the new or "better revelation," they claim. The Bible is starkly against such a premise. Thanks to the Holy Ghost, we understand that the scriptures are God-breathed (2 Timothy 3:16) and are of no private interpretation (2 Peter 1:20-21). That which God has said is forever settled in heaven (Psalm 119:89), and no angel in heaven has EVER been given the task or authority to explain, clarify, or contradict the word of God (Galatians 1:8-9). Like us, they can only declare what has already been written.

Chapter 2

The Enemy's Tactics

"Lest Satan should get an advantage of us: for we are not ignorant of his devices." (2 Corinthians 2:11KJV)

***

He Performs Lying Signs & Wonders:
The Spirit Of Anti-Christ

"The coming of the lawless one will be in accordance with how Satan works. He will use all sorts of displays of power through signs and wonders that serve the lie..." 2 Thessalonians 2:9 (NIV)

Jesus warns us in (Matthew 16:4 and Luke 11:29) that a wicked and perverse generation looks for signs and wonders. The keyword here is *"look,"* noting that these people demand to see *BEFORE* they believe. We, of course, believe in miracles because we believe in God. However, our belief is in GOD, not in miracles. Hebrews 11:3 says that it is "by faith we understand ." Jesus told his disciple, Thomas, "You believe because of what you have seen; blessed are those who have NOT seen and yet believe" (John 20:29 emphasis added).

In Deuteronomy 13:1-3 (KJV), we see God prioritizing commitment to Him above signs and wonders. *"If there arise among you a prophet, or a dreamer of dreams, and giveth thee a sign or a wonder, And the sign or the wonder come to pass, whereof he spake unto thee, saying, Let us go after other gods, which thou hast not known, and let us serve them; Thou shalt not hearken unto the words of that prophet, or that dreamer of dreams: for the Lord your God proveth you, to know whether ye love the Lord your God with all your heart and with all your soul."* The scriptures warn that we will have false teachers in our day, just as there were false prophets in the old days. The discerning factor of their ministry will be their teaching, not their exploits. God's leaders do everything to the glory of God, which includes how they live their lives and the principles they use to instruct ours. Faithful servants of God draw and focus our attention on God, not on them.

Satan Temps People To Sin

"But I fear, lest somehow, as the serpent deceived Eve by his craftiness, so your minds may be corrupted from the simplicity that is in Christ." 2 Corinthians 11:3 (KJV)

Sin (one's desire to please self) is intensified when Satan targets a weakness, an area of ignorance, or rebellion in our lives to cause us to give in to disobey God. God's requirement of us is simple: trust and obey his promises. However, sin separates us from God, feeding our impulse to provide for ourselves.

In Genesis 26:4, God promised Abraham that he would make his descents as the stars in the sky (innumerable). That is a great promise to believe, but the details must be left to God. However, the Bible shows in 1 Chronicles 21:1 that satan takes his role as the tempter of man - *"And Satan stood up against Israel, and provoked David to number Israel."*

Satan Plucks The Word of God Out of People's Hearts & Chokes Faith

"The sower soweth the word. And these are they by the way side, where the word is sown; but when they have heard, Satan cometh immediately, and taketh away the word that was sown in their hearts. And these are they likewise which are sown on stony ground; who, when they have heard the word, immediately receive it with gladness; And have no root in themselves, and so endure but for a time: afterward, when affliction or persecution ariseth for the word's sake, immediately they are offended. And these are they which are sown among thorns; such as hear the word, And the cares of this world, and the deceitfulness of riches, and the lusts of other things entering in, choke the word, and it becometh unfruitful. And these are they which are sown on good ground; such as hear the word, and receive it, and bring forth fruit, some thirtyfold, some sixty, and some an hundred." (Mark 4:14-20 KJV)

It gets no more precise than this. As a pastor, I sometimes feel this tactic is used most.

> Nothing chokes the word and sidetracks a believer like busyness and unfruitful conversations.

There have been times I have instructed those I've counseled or prayed for to go straight to their cars and head home immediately after a gathering. In addition to the state of your heart, I believe the company one keeps dramatically affects one's ability to retain the word of God. In such cases, I aim to give the Word of God time to catch root in the heart. Nothing chokes the word and sidetracks a believer like busyness and unfruitful conversations. Such things turn one's focus from the inward work God has begun in us to the external pursuits that will die away. If we are conscientious about guarding our hearts, we will find it easier to escape the strongholds from which we most desperately need deliverance.

Satan Causes Sickness & Disease

"So went Satan forth from the presence of the Lord, and smote Job with sore boils from the sole of his foot unto his crown." (Job 2:7 KJV)

As we will discover later, some physical ailments can be caused by evil spirits. Philippians 4:5 teaches that our self-discipline should be such that it is readily noticeable to others. Discipline in behavior and lifestyle keeps you fit and ready for God's use and better able to discern an unnatural attack on the body from a natural one. If you encounter an ailment that could not be caused by personal self-neglect, overindulgence, or environmental hazards, your struggle may not be with flesh and blood. Take heart by knowing that God is your covering. Just as Job had a hedge of protection, the enemy requires permission before interfering with our lives. Living within the boundaries of God's will prevents the enemy's unauthorized breaches.

Satan Fights Against The Laws of Ministry

"But if you bite and devour one another [in bickering and strife], watch out that you [along with your entire fellowship] are not consumed by one another." Galatians 5:15 (AMP)

I recall a sermon I preached called "Identity Crisis." This mentality causes Christians to live below their privilege in God, failing to realize who they are called to be in Christ. Understanding your identity informs you of how to function. Bickering and strife are countercultural, not to mention counterproductive to the Kingdom of God. 1 Peter 1:22 tells us that one of the tangible signs that God is working in your life is that you put away such behavior as you grow in the understanding of what Peter called, "unfeigned love of the brethren." Unfeigned means pure, sincere, authentic, or "unaffected." For a Christian to feel any other way than genuine love towards fellow believers and authentic leadership, there is a possibility that their heart may be "affected" by satan's influence in some way.

Paul states bluntly in Ephesians 2:2 that satan (the ruler of the power of the air) *is indeed at work in the sons of disobedience.* That is why we must constantly evaluate ourselves to remain in the faith (2 Corinthians 13:5). Check your actions and intentions to be sure they match your confession. If you find any contradictions, make no excuses for them, but pray the prayer of Psalm 86:11.

"Teach me thy way, O LORD; I will walk in thy truth: unite my heart to fear thy name." (Psalm 86:11KJV)

Satan Accuses Christians Before God

"And I heard a loud voice saying in heaven, Now is come salvation, and strength, and the kingdom of our God, and the power of his Christ: for the accuser of our brethren is cast down, which accused them before our God day and night." Revelation 12:10

Satan constantly accuses us before God in Heaven and our very hearts. His heavenly activity of accusation is depicted in the books of Job and Zechariah.

"Then Satan answered the Lord, and said, Doth Job fear God for naught? Hast not thou made an

*hedge about him, and about his house, and about
all that he hath on every side? thou hast blessed the
work of his hands, and his substance is increased in
the land. But put forth thine hand now, and touch
all that he hath, and he will curse thee to thy face."
Job 1:9-11 (KJV)*

*"Then the angel showed me Joshua the high priest
standing before the angel of the LORD, with Satan standing at his right hand to accuse him. And
the LORD said to Satan: "The LORD rebukes
you, Satan! Indeed, the LORD, who has chosen
Jerusalem, rebukes you! Is not this man a fire-
brand snatched from the fire?" Zechariah 3:1-2
(KJV)*

**Satan's attacks on the
Christian's conscience are
his last-ditch effort to make
us forfeit an already secured
victory.**

Every time satan challenges
God, he loses! To improve his
chances for success, he chal-
lenges us. The enemy focuses on those ignorant of their place
in God, tempting us to shrink back after every stumble or fall.
Satan's attacks on the Christian's conscience are his last-ditch
effort to make us forfeit an already secured victory. So when-

ever he accuses us in this way, we are encouraged by 1 John 2:1.

> *"My little children, these things write I unto you, that ye sin not. And if any man sin, we have an advocate with the Father, Jesus Christ the righteous:" (1 John 2:1 KJV)*

Chapter 3

How Spirits Transfer

—— ❈ ——

"Like a fluttering sparrow or a darting swallow, an undeserved curse will not land on its intended victim."
(Proverbs 26:2 NLT)

***

In 1995, my father pinned the initial work of this study. When discussing the topic of blessings and curses, he provided insight as to where curses come from. He defined it as follows:

> *In the scripture, we read about blessings and curses. Blessings are the result of obeying God, while curses are the result of obeying the devil. We are warned that the fathers' sins are visited upon the sons. As*

a result of the curse described in Genesis 3, Satan was given the power to strike out at mankind, and his demons were dispatched throughout the earth. Curses are brought on when someone willingly commits an act contrary to the Word of God. If demons have the right to remain with a person because of a curse, they cannot be cast out because of that curse. They likely will tell you that they have the right to remain. If a demon tells you it has a right to stay because of a curse, the curse must be broken for the demon to be cast out. *In the scriptures, we are warned that the father's sins are visited upon the third and fourth generations of those who disobey God (Genesis 20:5).*

As we discuss spiritual transfer in this chapter, we will see that there must first be an agreement before there can be an exchange of any kind. When money is transferred from one bank to another, a connection must first be established. When a student wishes to transfer from one institution to another, personal files must be shared. In every case of transfer, there is an established connection that must first be established.

Stand Guard At The Gates

"Watch over your heart with all diligence, for from it flow the springs of life." (Proverbs 4:23 AMP)

> *If a demon tells you it has a right to stay because of a curse, the curse must be broken for the demon to be cast out.*

What the Bible calls "the heart" can be regarded as the mind or soul. Almost everything we do in the body affects our soul, manifesting itself either mentally or emotionally. When it comes to guarding oneself against the enemy's influence, we must stand firm at the "Gates of The Five Senses."

The Eye Gate

"It doesn't hurt to look," says the husband, who consistently turns toward other women. Watching movies and videos showing pornography and murder opens the door to these spirits. When you preoccupy the mind with this activity, you open the door to temptation and lust. Jesus declared in Matthew 6:22-23 (NIV), *"The eye is the lamp of the body. If your eyes are healthy, your whole body will be full of light. But if your eyes are unhealthy, your whole body will be full of darkness. If then the light within you is darkness, how great is that darkness!"* Jesus taught that sins such as adultery do not start in the heart, they start with the eyes. We must be careful about what we allow our eyes to see. What we continuously look at sets the stage for what our hearts will dwell on.

The Ear Gate

Thousands of youth today are unaware of the power and influence of music. Across various genres, the mind becomes subject to subjective and explicit lyrics smuggled by the rhythmic or loud sounds that carry them. Music can open the door to many demons. In 2 Kings 17:17, the Bible mentions the people's use of enchantments. McClintock and Strongs Cyclopedia[1] references many Hebrew root words for enchantment; one of its definitions in Hebrew is the word *nachash'*, meaning to whisper a spell or *lut,* to muffle up, showing its broader original context and meaning. It is common practice for a music artist to pay top dollar for a soundtrack with a catchy beat, ensuring that his voice and message are played repeatedly. We will discuss more about music, specifically in Chapter 6.

---

1. https://www.biblicalcyclopedia.com/

The Nose Gate

Almost everything we do in the body affects our soul, manifesting itself either mentally or emotionally.

Many addictions endured in adulthood began with exposure during youth. Many youths are set down the road to addiction by smelling and inhaling unhealthy and illegal substances for the body. Like the tempting adulteress in Proverbs 7:17, psychological studies have tied a strong connection between the sense of smell and its ability to incite strong desire, hunger, or nostalgia. This can be seen in how cologne or perfume reminds us of people and places. Some people have an affinity for the use of oils and incents, attributing to them the additional attribute of altering a person's mood or atmosphere. Others go as far as to practice the burning of herbs such as sage as a method to ward off evil spirits. The weapons of our spiritual warfare are not carnal but spiritual. All such attempts, whether they be mystical or medicinal, are simply an attempt to solve a spiritual problem by natural means.

The Mouth Gate

Excessive eating and drinking - gluttony as the Bible calls it, is a wide-open door to the demonic realm (Proverbs 23:20-23, 29-30, Proverbs 20:1). In many cases, uncontrol in this area is usually an indicator of some frustration or torment we are seeking ease from. Likewise, certain things that come out of the mouth (profanity, blasphemy, etc.) make way for demons (Proverbs 18:21, James 3:9-12). We can invite undesirable things and people into our lives by the use of careless conversations or harsh joking.

The Touch Gate

I want to categorize "touch" into three areas:

- _Violence & Murder:_ (Isaiah 59:6-9, Proverbs 16:29) God deeply disdains violence. Man's violence grieved God to the point of repentance in Noah's day (Genesis 6:5-7), and of course, satan has been a murderer from the beginning (John 8:44).

- _Associated Company/Covenants:_ In Mathew 18:19 (KJV), Jesus taught how our collaborative activity is as potent and binding as physical touch; _"Again I say unto you, That if two of you shall _agree_ on earth as _touching_ anything that they shall ask, it shall be done for them of my Father which is in heaven" (emphasis added)._ The positive impact of this principle Jesus shows here is balanced by the wise warnings of proverbs regarding agreeing with the "wrong people" (Proverbs 1:10).

As global community members, we must understand the difference between a contract and a covenant. Many cultures and communities have different names for them, but their operating principles are very much the same. A contract is a written or spoken agreement about a particular person, product, or service to be performed for a specific fee over a predetermined time, such as employment, sales, or tenancy. Contracts are usually enforceable by law and limited exclusively to previously defined terms and conditions. Contracts are intended to aid two or more parties in determining how they will work together in good faith.

Most importantly, a contract is limitedly binding. Most employment contracts, for instance, operate under "At Will" employment law. At any time, a company or employee can terminate their working relationship without explanation or retaliation. On the other hand, a covenant is much broader and ambiguous in its scope and more profound in its meaning. Covenant derives from the same root word meaning "to cut," usually involving the use or identifying factor of blood. We see a positive example of this in the institution of marriage between a man and woman and the definition of salvation provided by Jesus Christ to an individual believer. A marriage covenant changes the priority and focus of an individual's entire life (Matthew 19:5-6). In like manner, Jesus Christ requires his disciples to become dead to the things of the world so that their entire life reflects the glory of their savior (Luke 14:26-33). These are the only two covenants Jesus endorses; in both cases, he urges us to consider them seriously. In all other agreements, Jesus tells us never to go beyond letting our "yes" be "yes" and our "no" be "no" (Matthew 5:37). Anything beyond this is of the evil one.

- *Sensuality/Sex:* Intimate touching of another body outside of marriage is forbidden by God. When a person engages in illicit sex, they sin against their own body (1 Corinthians 6:18). Sex opens the door for demons to enter (1 Corinthian 6:16).

As you can see, negative/unholy spirits can transfer. The transmission of wicked spirits can occur when a connection or agreement is made with any object or person under demonic influence or control. The untainted person involved is at risk of contamination when exposed to these persons or things acting as gates of influence for evil spirits. This principle is illustrated clearly in Joshua 6:18 NKJV; *"And you, by all means abstain from the accursed things, lest you become accursed when you take of the accursed things, and make the camp of Israel a curse, and trouble it."*

Here, I have laid out only a few examples of how spirits can be transferred, positively or negatively. satan and his co-

> *The transmission of wicked spirits can occur when a connection or agreement is made with any object or person under demonic influence or control.*

horts are the originators and initiators of these negative transferences, and they work through people to accomplish their goals. Over the years, I have encountered many people who could not explain why their home life, working environment, or family dynamic was in disarray. Spirits are real, so consider this guide carefully, for as the scriptures warn, *"no curse comes without a cause"* (Proverbs 26:2). Consider even the various regional or national landscapes worldwide; you can track cultural trends that emulate recklessness, immorality, anger, pride, materialism, hatred, etc.

Laying Of Hands

There is a powerful transference that occurs through the laying of hands. The Holy Bible tells us in Deuteronomy 34:9 that through "the positive" laying of hands, Prophet Moses transferred the spirit of wisdom unto Joshua, enabling him to lead the Israelites to the promised land. This transference was necessary due to God's decision to call Moses home *(by death)* following a severe lapse in judgment due to Moses' anger. Jesus provides further insight into this practice through his ministry example recorded in Matthew 9:27-29:

> *"After Jesus left the girl's home, two blind men followed along behind him, shouting, "Son of David, have mercy on us! They went right into the house where he was staying, and Jesus asked them, "Do you believe I can make you see? 'Yes, Lord,' they told him, 'we do.' Then he touched their eyes and said, "Because of your faith, it will happen."* (Matthew 9:27-29 NLT)

Notice how Jesus first asked the blind men if they "believed." They answered yes while calling him "Lord," signifying their agreement and submission to Jesus' authority concerning their life and health. This gives power and significance to the laying on of hands, which Hebrews 6:1-2 calls "foundational." When you participate in this act of faith, you declare with your actions your acknowledgment and willing submission to the faith and commission of the one laying hands. *"And without question, the person who has the power to give a blessing is greater than the one who is blessed"* (Hebrews 7:7 NLT).

As demonstrated in the life and ministry of Moses and Jesus, the principle and practice of laying hands continued through the church age. Paul reminded Timothy to stir up the gift he had received through the laying of Paul's hands (2 Timothy 1:6).

With every principle or law, there is a negative reality to it as well. When done incorrect-

Contact with these "contaminated hands" for one reason or another can bring about great agony to an individual or family.

ly, such "touching in agreement" can be destructive outside of God's leading. Through the adverse application of laying hands, many can suffer a great deal as a result. Contact with these "contaminated hands" for one reason or another can bring about great agony to an individual or family. This may sound alarming and foreboding to some, but take courage; God's grace is sufficient. God's children walk in the light (truth). In doing so, we can be trusting and discerning. We must always be fully armed against the daily attacks of the enemy. It is our lack of knowledge that satan depends on to gain an advantage over us. Ignorance is no excuse from the laws of spiritual warfare. Everyone must not willingly or ignorantly participate in things that solicit ungodly participation (e.g., witch doctors, mediums, occultic practices, marine agents, false doctrine[2Peter 2:1], and evil people in general).

Words or Communications

"Do not be misled: Bad company corrupts good character." (1 Corinthians 15:33 NIV)

Be sure to select your close friends among Christian believers only; even then, do so wisely. Exposure to immoral behavior or communication can corrupt anyone, no matter how wise or mature they may be. The "ear gate," as I call it, is a chief entryway to the soul. Hebrews 11 is clear in teaching that faith comes by hearing. What we hear shapes our understanding, affects our emotions, and dictates our faith level in God or something else.

Suppose a person is having regular communication (in person, by phone, or by text) with someone who is generally negative in their thoughts about life, immoral in their actions, or overly critical of people. It is only a matter of time before the person who continues to listen to such things is negatively affected. They must be cut off, no matter who they are to you. When presenting this scenario, I often encounter resistance from those who somehow feel obligated to those they are socially connected with. My reply to such an objection is this.

Who is better positioned for you to have "unguarded" conversations with than those you call a friend or family member? As stated before, the purpose here is not for us to become distrustful but discerning. The power of spoken words has an incredible effect on the human mind.

The inward change brought about in the soul by spoken word is rarely instantaneous as

> *Who is better positioned for you to have "unguarded" conversations with than those you call a friend or family member?*

one would suppose, looking superficially upon an individual's momentary reply or the crowd's corporate response. It's the "continuous hearing" that will either build or destroy the faith of God in our lives. That's why scriptures such as (Psalm 1:2 and Joshua 1:8) emphasize repetition when it comes to the word of God and its ability to cause lasting effects on our lives. In the same way, prolonged exposure to negative thoughts and words may not immediately yield outward changes in behavior, but the inward corrosion is progressive. External behavior change soon follows, as the damning consequences of inner convictions erode over time as the surrounding godless clamor takes its toll.

All such "talk" comes from the "Strange Woman" (False Wisdom) described in Proverbs 5. She is not to be confused with the "Adulteress Woman" of Proverbs 7-9. "The adulteress" chiefly represents sensual and sexual vices. The "Strange Woman" is the voice that rails against all wisdom and discretion. The "strange woman" of Proverbs 5 represents the voice of the gossip, false teacher, and fake friend who would sooner lead you astray rather than lead you to bed.

Proverbs 5:1-5 (KJV) says, *"My son, attend unto my wisdom, and bow thine ear to my understanding: That thou mayest regard discretion, and that thy lips may keep knowledge. For the lips of a strange woman drop as an honeycomb, and her mouth is smoother than oil: But her end is bitter as wormwood, sharp as a two-edged sword. Her feet go down to death; her steps take hold on hell."* This warning is more prevalent today than ever. The Apostle Paul told Timothy that people would one day depart from the faith. They would fall away because they would be unable to endure sound doctrine. They will instead be led away by seductive spirits that will teach them devilish doctrines.

Mind Your Associations

Mind the people and circles in which you move or associate. Take marriage, for example; the union between believers and unbelievers should be discouraged. In such stark contrasts in personal belief and lifestyle, a connection between two individuals is forbidden in scripture. The intent is to prevent someone from being contaminated or hindered by another (2 Corinthians 6:14-18). Concerning marriage, this advice is directed to those still single and free to choose their partner. Guidance concerning those who have come to Christ after marriage is an entirely different matter that we will not unpack here. To begin reading on this subject, please see (1Peter 3:1-2 and 1 Corinthians 7:10-14).

Whenever it is within your power to do so, believers should move in the company of consecrated believers. I can recall many scenarios in which good people took a turn for the worse because of negative associations. It's heartbreaking to see once "stable," well-meaning people undergo such a character change. The effect of bad company is corrosive; the humble and harmless begin to parade as hired killers, drug peddlers, drunkards, and cheats. Sincerity gives way to immorality, and the imagination is progressively filled with deceit and distrust. Passive or active agreement in bad behavior brings about corruption because of the behavior modeled by these "new kinds of friends."

Mind the people and circles in which you move or associate.

"As iron sharpens iron, so a friend sharpens a friend" (Proverbs 27:17 NLT).

The Bible declares plainly what sociological research has repeatedly reported. In essence, "You are who you hang around." There is no secret as to why close friends typically share the same salary within a $5-10k range. A student often hangs out and studies with those with similar or greater GPAs and career goals. Sports dynasties and business industry leaders continue to win year after year, a credit to their ability to acquire and maintain a continuous roster of top talent. Having the right people around you is essential to your success. The opposite is also true, often with catastrophic results. My father always said, *"If you have nine broke friends long enough, you will become the tenth."* Proverbs 13:20 KJV says, "He that walketh with wise men shall be wise: but a companion of fools shall be destroyed."

Subtle connections can lead to sudden results:

The Good

- Elisha received a double portion of Elijah's life anointing in 1 day because of the relationship and proximity he maintained with him for six years (2 Kings 2:9-11).

- Within three years, followers graduated to friends through their relationship with Jesus Christ (John 15:14-16).

The Bad

- God held the entire nation of Israel responsible for sin because of one man among them who secretly kept goods that were consecrated to the Lord (Joshua Chapter 7)

- Jacob's new wife, Rachel, secretly kept the idolatrous practices of her family without Jacob's knowledge. Her secret association in this way gave Jacob's enemy (her father) valid cause to pursue and accuse him of theft. (Genesis 31:19, 29-32)

Sex

There is a powerful transference that occurs through sex and one of the easiest ways to transfer spirits from one person to another. In most cases, the spiritual transference is negative when sexual activity is illicit. The Bible tells us in 1 Corinthians 6:16 that you become one if you are joined sexually with a harlot. The universal principle of sexual union is as clear as Genesis 4:1. However, the strong language used in Corinthians 6:16 is not without reason. The contrasting illustration of the "harlot" sexually involved with a "believer" teaches us two things.

1. <u>The union is instant and spiritually unsafe</u>: *"Do you not know that he who unites himself with a prostitute is one with her in body? For it is said, "The two will become one flesh" (NIV).* The oneness of flesh begins the moment the two unite. Fundamentally, sexual intercourse (protected or not) is not without the exchange of bodily fluids. This degree of physical exposure puts one at a much higher medical risk, creating additional openings for spiritual influence and strongholds.

- Romans 1:27 alludes to the "unshielded consequences" that abnormal body use can bring. For instance, take notice of the number of diseases and infections one can contract exclusively through sexual contact.

- Luke 13:11 and Matthew 8:16 show that some physical ailments are spiritual in origin, though they manifest naturally through sickness. Staying physically pure is our first line of defense in staying healthy and spiritually free.

2. <u>Long-term exposure is NOT required for long-term effects:</u>

Paul's reference to the "prostitute/harlot" was not merely a spiritual allegory for idolatry but also a practical example of how our human nature is prone to entertain sin. We flirt with it, play with it, and may decide to spend a night or two with it to see if it's worth the talk we've heard. "We're not that serious," "I'm still young," "It's only sex." The enemy wants you to believe these rationalizations and other such lies. However, the truth is that it only takes a 30-second glance to rob you of the next 30 years of your life (Proverbs 7:21-23). In this life, we all have to fight through temptations, but for sexual sin, we are instructed to run (1 Corinthians 6:18).

Mark 5:9 KJV says, *"And he asked him, What is thy name? And he answered, saying, My name is Legion: for we are many."* Now, can you imagine if you have a sexual relationship with a highly demonized person(s) or a member of the occult? A witch or wizard, a fetish priest, or a marine agent? Such a union will bring an unholy transference of spirits from such a person to the unsuspecting victim. Such transferences have resulted in some men and women becoming barren, impotent, infertile, and backward in their endeavors. Another disheartening consequence is when people lose control over their sexual appetite to the extent that they cannot sleep one night without having sex. For singles, this can delay them from getting married on time. Those involved in sexual perversions such as homosexuality, bestiality, incest, oral and anal sex practices, and excessive and indiscriminate sexual acts endanger their lives. People engaged in evil (especially together) can open doors for the unholy transference of spirits (Lev. 20:13), leading to unholy soul ties.

Chapter 4

Media & Culture

"The light of the body is the <u>eye</u>: if therefore thine eye be single (holy), thy whole body shall be full of light. But if thine eye be evil, thy whole body shall be full of darkness. "If therefore the light that is in thee be darkness, how great is that darkness!"
(Matthew 6:22-23 KJV emphasis added).

***

Television

Without a doubt, we ought to watch what we eat or, in this case, "consume." The role of visual media today has become a powerful one. In a businessinsider.com article,

Ivan De Luce cited some astounding numbers. *According to the 2019 Ad Age Leading National Advertisers report*[1]*, the top 200 advertisers collectively spent $163 billion on advertising in 2018. Some of the most significant ad spending increases came from internet-based giants like Amazon (32%), Google (23%), and Facebook (236%).*

There is a reason companies (especially those in the US) spend billions of dollars on commercials and strategically place their products inside of our favorite movie scenes and TV shows: because it works. Years of consumer behavior data and consumer debt show that companies have no problems playing this game because they are winning.

One can only turn on their television or mobile device to see that we are constantly fed a stream of "immortality." The routine coverage of criminal atrocities, mature-rated story-lines, or the suggestive innuendo of ad commercials conditions us. The influence of immorality (like sin in general) has an eroding effect on one's convictions. Moral erosion can usually happen subtly over time or suddenly through "shock and awe" tactics found in news media, movies, or high-profile

---

1. https://adage.com/article/datacenter/ad-age-leading-na
tional-advertisers-2019-index/2178026

commercial ads. The examples mentioned earlier are just the tip of the iceberg. Take, for instance, the political bend behind many news outlets, expertly using our fears and biases to manipulate public opinion. Every year, many Americans tune in or attend Superbowl watch parties strictly for the commercials. Seemingly, every year, these new commercials redraw the lines for age-appropriate sexuality or the definition of success. There is always a certain degree of shock value in commercials. Advertisers only have 30 seconds to capture your attention and win your opinion.

On the other hand, sitcoms (situational comedies) have 30 minutes daily or weekly to use "creative license" in disseminating various ideas with humor or flippancy—a very effective tool when challenging conventional thought or belief systems. Comedic satire is the perfect breeding ground for posing rhetorical questions, using suggestive language, and provocative scenarios within a context of cultural undertones that work to desensitize us by normalizing destructive ideals we are warned about in the Bible. Since the advent of the printing press, the ever-evolving impact of mass media communication is undeniable and has yielded significant benefits in many ways. Like any tool, it is an extension of the worker that wields it. The enemy has deliberately degraded the compass of our moral standards through years of planned programs.

> *"Everything is wearisome beyond description. No matter how much we see, we are never satisfied. No matter how much we hear, we are not content."*
> (Ecclesiastes 1:8 NLT)

We must be guided by God's word in determining what is best for us. Ecclesiastes shares a startling observation in verse eight. Unlike the stomach, the eyes and ears will never alert you to the danger of overconsumption. Ecclesiastes says that the eye and the ear will never be tired of doing what they do. The inability of the ear and eye to be filled makes us exceptionally vulnerable to moral decay and slaves to addiction and our impulse triggers. When we expose the eye and ear gate to pornographic, lude, or abusive content, we quietly sow contrary seeds (tares) in our hearts and minds. In Mark 4:14-20, Jesus likened the heart to that of soil. Whatever you allow into your heart (ground) will indiscriminately "by nature" produce manifold fruit.

> *Unlike the stomach, the eyes and ears will never alert you to the danger of over consumption.*

Don't be misled—you cannot mock the justice of God. You will always harvest what you plant. Those who live only to satisfy their sinful nature will harvest decay and death from that sinful nature. But those who live to please the Spirit will harvest everlasting life from the Spirit. (Galatians 6:7-8 NLT)

The "kingdom of darkness" is built on counterfeits: the Bible clarifies that "the wages of sin is death." As a pastor, I often worry that most people are too "carnal-minded" even when considering spiritual matters. Just as Eve was deceived in the garden, I fear many of us think only of an immediate physical death when flirting with sin's promises. However, I've come to learn that sin's wages can pay out in a variety of ways, all of which are spiritually lethal; however, some are not immediately perceptible to its victim (1 John 5:17). Hebrews 3:13 speaks on the deceitfulness of sin; because we don't see an immediate, physical act of judgment such as loss of life or pain, we somehow begin to believe that God is not aware or decides not to hold us accountable for the choices we make. The truth is, sin's wages are paid and with great regularity.

We cannot anticipate the form those wages take in our lives. Immorality in any form, if left unchecked, will undoubtedly

What may have begun as a private pet sin eventually spreads - killing relationships, reputations, and trust.

spring up and defile other areas of life. What may have begun as a private pet sin eventually spreads - killing relationships, reputations, and trust. God was the first to understand the importance of "television" programming. For God to get the word in the hearts of his people, he kept His word constantly in their vision.

"These commandments that I give you today are to be on your hearts. Impress them on your children. Talk about them when you sit at home and when you walk along the road when you lie down, and when you get up. Tie them as symbols on your hands and bind them on your foreheads. Write them on the doorframes of your houses and on your gates." (Deuteronomy 6:6-9 NIV)

"Fix these words of mine in your hearts and minds; tie them as symbols on your hands and bind them on your foreheads. Teach them to your chil-

dren, talking about them when you sit at home and when you walk along the road, when you lie down and when you get up. Write them on the doorframes of your houses and on your gates" *(Deuteronomy 11:18-20 NIV)*

The same holds today as The "Holy Spirit" is transmitted to us by watching programs that encourage the "soaking in" of the Word of God along with praise and worship devoted to God. Similarly, "unclean spirits" seek to set up strongholds by erecting thoughts and mental pictures that inflame our desires and act as barriers to the knowledge of God (2 Corinthians 10:5). That is why it is so important to God that we guard our hearts with all diligence. The enemy works to quench our discernment by convincing us that such things are not serious at all. That it's nothing but "entertainment," and you would "never" seriously act on such ideas. Paul warns against such reasoning, knowing full well what the end will be. 2 Corinthians 11:3 (NKJV) says, *"But I fear, lest somehow, as the serpent deceived Eve by his craftiness, so your minds may be corrupted from the simplicity that is in Christ."* This threat still exists, so be on your guard. Just as God gave His "tele-vision program" in Deuteronomy, the people of God had utterly "changed channels" by Isaiah's day.

"You have put up your false gods behind the door on the other side. You have turned away from Me and have taken the covering off yourself. You have gone up and made your bed wide. You have made an agreement for yourselves with them. You have loved their bed and have looked upon their [naked] bodies." (Isaiah 57:8 NLV emphasis added)

Books

Just as the Holy Spirit is transferred through the Holy Bible's reading, evil spirits can be transferred quickly by reading occultic, pornographic, or abusive material. Such material finds its entryway by appealing to one's pride or desire for a particular objective. Be it subtlety or blatantly, authors of such material find a way to glorify or glamorize ideas and images that can be lude, violent, abusive, at best, spiritually cloudy, and unsupported by scripture. As "enlightened" as these authors of error claim to be, the common thread of all such deceptive work is PRIDE. The enemy uses pride to anchor us to an attraction or intent driven by a base desire. Let's take the writing genre of erotica; for example, on its covers, you may sometimes find suggestive images of half-naked men and women engaging in what could be described as "acts of passion." These cover pages, however, are just that, suggestive covers. The "real danger" is found in the literature it contains.

Such writing creates and builds upon a thirst for fantasy using mental imagery that "real life" is not meant to support. This problem is increased 10x through the audiovisual stimuli of erotic or pornographic videos. The word pornography is the amalgamation of two Greek words, "Porni" (prostitute) and "graphein" (to write), loosely translated to mean *the writings of a prostitute.*" These erotica novels do not include any pictures beyond the scanty romance cover, so it is more widely tolerated or rated "PG," making them commonplace among the higher shelves of the magazine stand and the reading section at the grocery store. Most shoppers don't visit the grocery store for its "reading selection," yet very few can resist the urge to browse the tabloids while standing in the check-out line.

"Then [Jesus] added, "<u>Pay close attention to what you hear</u>. The closer you listen, the more understanding you will be given—and you will receive even more. (Mark 4:24 NLT emphasis added)

Be on your guard also as you engage in the pursuit of knowledge. Growing in knowledge and understanding is good: the Bible encourages us to do so. Despite the apparent benefits of "gaining knowledge," gaining wisdom is the "principal thing" (Proverbs 4:7).

The Bible warns that information alone can be dangerous, making one susceptible to vanity and pride, for "knowledge puffs up" (1 Corinthians 8:1). I continually encourage my ministers with the words of 2Timothy 2:15 (KJV) - "*Study to shew thyself approved unto God, a workman that needeth not to be ashamed, rightly dividing the word of truth.*" It is essential for every saint of God, especially ministers, to study the Bible continuously while reading broadly, but we must be careful when doing so.

Many deceptions are hidden in what is considered generally accepted cultural practices.

What makes satan and his agents so dangerous is their "subtlety and craftiness" (Acts 13:10). We must heed no other voice but God and his word for our life's direction. Colossians 2:20-23 acknowledges that we will encounter many different philosophies, regiments, and principles (of this world). Some of these regiments may have (in part) some natural benefits but are only partially trustworthy. You can find many nuggets of misinformation crouched in popular themes like The Law of Attraction, some Health & Wellness, Yoga, some Business Leadership practices, or other New-age inspirational/Motivational techniques. Paul warned Timothy not to be deceived by such "destructive arguments" and the supposed objective stances they misleadingly represent. The enemy often uses such things as a Trojan Horse to transfer his demonic influence under the guise of "science -falsely so-called" (1 Timothy 6:20-21). Many deceptions are hidden in what is considered generally accepted cultural practices.

Chapter 5

Generational Curses

———— ⬥ ————

"And shewing mercy unto thousands of them that love me, and keep my commandments." (Exodus 20:6)

***

Parents & Family

L et's deal with a real issue that is affecting all of us. We don't like to talk about it, but it is necessary if we are to overcome it. Generational Curses are the reoccurring problems, the traceable patterns in our families. These reoccurring patterns steal, kill, and destroy the progress of our lives in whole or in part. These curses manifest patterns of rejection, instability, abuse, and other oppressions brought on by demonic powers that plague countless families. This is separate from the expected trials that come with the seasons of life. Instead, a family could be under demonic assault at the hands of a family curse revisiting a new generation. As we will see, such could be inherited because of the sins of our ancestors.

> *...a family could be under demonic assault at the hands of a family curse...*

We see how the physical characteristics of parents are passed to their children. We adore newborns with phrases like, "She has her mother's eyes." or "He looks just like his father." Whether You've received your big nose from your dad or your mother's smile, that might not be the only thing they gave you. Just as you may be physically short, tall, light-skinned, or dark-skinned, much of who you are is significantly influenced by heredity.

Heredity has advantages, blessing us with talents, abilities, and unique traits. However, the opposite can be confirmed in hereditary's ability to inform how you think and behave, especially if those frameworks are counterproductive to us. This gives new weight to the common expression, "Like father, like son." Unbeknownst to some, the same rings true in the spiritual realm. Generational influences can bring either blessings or curses to your life. Understanding this reality gives us the power to improve our lives as individuals and families.

Family is important to God. We see in scripture how God doesn't just deal with man individually but generationally. Matthew 1:17 tells us: "So all the generations from Abraham to David are fourteen generations, from David until the captivity in Babylon are fourteen generations, and from the captivity in Babylon until the Christ are fourteen generations." When God looks at you, He also sees your family, where you came from, and what you struggle with. At the same time, he sees your potential. Looking at you, He can see your ancestors, children, and grandchildren.

When God looks at you, He also sees your family, where you came from, and what you struggle with.

When making a covenant with Abraham, God did not promise to bless him alone. He always said, "I will bless you and your descendants." An example of this is in Genesis 22:17-18, where God said, "In blessing, I will bless you, and multiplying I will multiply your descendants as the stars of the heaven and as the sand which is on the seashore; and your descendants shall possess the gate of their enemies. In your seed, all the nations of the earth shall be blessed because you have obeyed My voice." Abraham obeyed God and was blessed. His actions established a covenant with God through which his descendants were also blessed. Covenant blessings can also be seen through bloodlines. These are what I call generational blessings.

Curses also run along bloodlines. In Exodus 20:5-6, God warns the children of Israel not to follow false gods, saying, "You shall not bow down to them nor serve them. For I, the Lord your God, am a jealous God, visiting the iniquity of the fathers upon the children to the third and fourth generations of those who hate Me, but showing mercy to thousands, to those who love Me and keep My commandments."

What makes generational curses unique is the pattern of iniquity that enables the hin-

Covenant blessings can be seen through bloodlines.

dering sin of a family line. The word "iniquity" means to be bent. In this context, to be inclined towards a particular sin, we see that the iniquity of the parents is carried on to the children of the third and fourth generations. This means a child will be bent like their parents, grandparents, and great-grandparents, having the same inner inclination toward certain sinful habits. Lamentations 5:7 says, *"Our fathers sinned and are no more, but we bear their iniquities."* In other words, even though they may be dead and buried, the iniquity of their life remains with you like a family heirloom. Deuteronomy 28:15-68 contains fifty-three verses listing generational curses. Here are just a few of the "symptoms" listed below which are the result of the curse:

Symptoms

Poverty Mental Illness Sexual Abuse/Perversion Child Abuse Depression	Hereditary Disease Suicide Divorce Anxiety/Panic attacks Immorality Destructive Attitudes & Behaviors	Adultery Domestic Violence Addiction Alcoholism/Drugs Fear Indecision/Compulsion

Deuteronomy 28:1-14 consists of what my church and I call "the blessing plan."Often, we would use verses 1-14 as a congregational reading. During a teaching session where I expounded on the remaining verses in the chapter, the curses seemed rather lopsided compared to the first 14 verses. I often asked, *"Why so many curses?"*

Jesus best answers this question in Matthew 7:13-14, *"Enter through the narrow gate. For wide is the gate and broad is the road that leads to destruction, and many enter through it. But small is the gate and narrow the road that leads to life, and only a few find it."*

The Bible does not suggest that all of these things will happen to every disobedient person all at once; instead, the warning is that any number of these things can happen. One curse is more than enough to destroy someone with very little help from the other curses. A short survey of Deuteronomy 28:15-68 will show that any one or two of those cursed situations is enough to ruin a life. *Broad is the way to destruction*, which means that there are many different ways to be destroyed, but only one way to be saved. The Lord urges us to choose life so that we and our seed may live (Deuteronomy 30:19). Despite the generational consequences of such curses, every individual and every generation is given a choice. Every one of us is liable to be bothered by the choices of those who came before us, but we do not have to be bound. God gives us all a chance to choose life and live.

To battle through any of the above-listed issues does not automatically mean there is a generational curse somewhere, but Deuteronomy lists these consequences for a reason. Note that all have their root cause of iniquity, of which we need God to stay free. While you may or may not be a victim of a generational curse, we must remain obedient to God's word, or else we may become the starting cause of one. Your future depends on your choices.

Many people, if not most, can identify with some of these symptoms passed on from previous generations. When you look at your family tree, do you see a pattern linking to any of these things?

A single act of disobedience can set off "patterns of iniquity." Actions initiated long be-

> Broad is the way to destruction means that there are many different ways to be destroyed, but only one way to be saved.

fore a person is born can create environments that shape a group or family's convictions and life patterns that imprison members of the following generation to repeat those same patterns and norms terminally. These crippling behaviors and beliefs, modeled before us as children, teach us to color dysfunction as "normal" as adults. It is not uncommon for children who were abused in their youth to grow up and become perpetrators of pain. The formation and perpetuation of spiritual strongholds can be passed down from what the Bible describes as *"the tradition of our fathers."* Regarding dysfunctional families, learned behavior through conditioning or acute exposure can result in prolonged trauma.

Social Conditioning

"He answered and said unto them, Well hath Esaias prophesied of <u>you hypocrites</u>, as it is written,

This people honoureth me with their lips, but their heart is far from me. Howbeit in vain do they worship me, teaching for doctrines the commandments of men. For laying aside the commandment of God, ye hold the tradition of men, as the washing of pots and cups: and many other such like things ye do. And he said unto them, Full well <u>ye reject the commandment of God, that ye may keep your own tradition.</u> (Mark 7:6-10 emphasis added)

The Family Ham

My father often told a story about a woman who showed her young daughter how to prepare the family ham one day. She would walk her through all of the preparations and ingredients. When she explained how to prepare the ham before putting it in the oven, the mother clarified to her daughter that they would ALWAYS cut the two ends off the ham before putting it into the pot. The daughter asked her mother why was cutting the ham in this way so important. The mother didn't answer but reiterated that cutting the two ends off the ham was the way to do it.

Eventually, the mother also became curious about the purpose of cutting the ham, because she never understood why.

She called her mother and was determined to discover the secret behind cutting the two ends off the ham. When she got ahold of her mother, she asked again why it was so important that the two ends of the ham had to be cut. Her mother replied. I had a small pan. The only way the ham could fit was to cut the two ends. All this time, without understanding the original intent, a tradition that had no value beyond the generation it was meant to help was continually taught, practiced, and passed down.

Some tradition is good, while others can be crippling. Especially practices that God did not ordain or those that do not help people honor and worship God in spirit and truth. Jesus talked about such "traditions" when he quoted Elisha in Mark chapter 7. Those traditions are the most dangerous of all, though they tend to appear religious. There are few strongholds more potent than the superstitious or self-righteous kind. They are two sides of the same coin called idolatry. No matter how noble the intent of an initial practice or action may have been (for I believe many practices often begin sincerely), along the way, a believer can fall in love with a person, place, or preference of worship—over time, the object, individual, or preference of worship hinders the hearing of God's voice (Matthew 17:3-5).

Jesus still speaks today, as he said in John 8:37-44. Jesus challenged a group of Jews with a call for self-examination. In today's language, many justify their actions by claiming they are doing what "grandma would have done ." In more religious settings, some assume doctrinal dominance based on their tenure, being brought up in the "old school traditions" that were started by great men and women of God from yesterday. Let's take a closer look at John 8:39-40.

> *"They answered and said unto him, Abraham is our father. Jesus saith unto them, If ye were Abraham's children, ye would do the works of Abraham. But now ye seek to kill me, a man that hath told you the truth, which I have heard of God: this did not Abraham." (John 8:39-40 KJV)*

The danger of tradition is the damage that can occur when practice is kept, but the spirit is lost.

In the same way today, such arguments stake their claim on the superficial while voiding the faith that made their historical connection special. Though Jesus' adversaries had legitimate family ties to Abraham, Jesus calls them out on their faith and character, being nothing like Abraham's. The danger of tradition is the damage that can occur when practice is kept, but the spirit is lost. Those who maintain only the routine lose the revelation God gave those who began in spirit and truth. So, generation after generation passes on the work, while the worship is long forgotten. These golden calves can be found all around us. We would do well to examine ourselves to eliminate them wherever they may be, whether in our homes or hearts.

> *"...And remember that the heavenly Father to whom you pray has no favorites. He will judge or reward you according to what you do. So you must live in reverent fear of him during your time here as 'temporary residents.' For you know that God paid a ransom to save you from the empty life you inherited from your ancestors. And it was not paid with mere gold or silver, which lose their value. It was the precious blood of Christ, the sinless, spotless Lamb of God. God chose him as your ransom long before the world began, but now in these last days, he has been revealed for your sake".(*1 Peter 1:17-20 NLT)

This should bring you great joy in knowing that you are not bound to your past but delivered from it all if you belong entirely to Christ. I do not wish to raise concern, but rather your awareness of the fullness of God's grace, which has been made available to us through Christ Jesus our Lord.

Dysfunctional Families

The term dysfunctional is used quite often today concerning families. The word refers to the sense of disintegration produced in a family with many hurts. From a Christian perspective, it is a home that is not functioning as God intended. It could result from divorce, lack of communication, rivalry among the children, self-consumed parents, addictions, child abuse, sexual abuse, spousal abuse, extramarital affairs, pornography, etc. One of the strange dynamics in family life is that when children grow up, they often repeat the behaviors of their families. The truth is, what we know about marriage and parenting, for good or bad, we learn from what was modeled in our homes. The result is that dysfunctional families can often create dysfunctional families for generations. This is part of what the Bible speaks of in Numbers 14:18, "God visits the iniquity of the fathers on the children to the third and fourth generation." Living in such a family can make it very difficult to live for God, but it's not impossible, as we will see.

Joseph is proof that break-ing a generational curse can be done. Joseph was raised in a

...dysfunctional families can often create dysfunctional families for generations.

home filled with angry, jealous, and deceitful people, yet he became one of the two men whose lives are recorded in the Bible about whom there is not one word of criticism. Joseph was faithful in an imperfect family, and we want to examine his life today and see what insights we can gain for our own lives. Jacob, Joseph's father, was a polygamist and a passive parent who openly favored his children. Jacob was grossly passive as a parent. Earlier great tragedy had befallen the family; as they traveled across the country, Jacob's daughter was raped by the son of the mayor of Shechem (Genesis 34:1-2). When Jacob learned what had happened, he did nothing. However, when they saw that their father would do nothing, the sons took matters into their own hands. They devised a plan and killed all the men in the city (Genesis 34:29).

When Jacob learned what they had done, his chief concern was avoiding a bad reputation with the rest of the people in the land. Still, he did nothing! Later, his oldest son, Reuben, had a sexual affair with Bilhah, his concubine (Genesis 35:21). When he learned of Dinah's rape, he did nothing; when Jacob learned his sons were guilty of murder, he did nothing. When Jacob realized that his son had committed incest, he still did nothing. It is hard to calculate how Jacob's passiveness as a parent contributed to the turmoil in this family. Jacob is a classic illustration of a man who may be preoccupied, unconcerned, or too busy to lead his family. Jacob was too passive to deal with what was occurring in the lives of any of his children.

Jacob was passive in his parenting, and his children had watched as he played favorites with Joseph for seventeen years. Genesis 37:3 says, "Now Israel loved Joseph more than all his children because he was the son of his old age." Joseph, now seventeen, was the first-born son of his father's favorite wife, Rachel. According to scripture, Joseph was born to his father late in life. There are some valid reasons why the baby of the family, especially the one born late in the parents' life, is favored. Most parents are more relaxed and easygoing with these children because they have learned from their previous parenting experiences.

Another cause of the relaxed parenting approach is that the parents are more adjusted to their marital relationship. Furthermore, the parents are often better economically to give the younger child more advantages. No matter the reason for the benefits provided to the younger child, they can create jealousy in the older child or children.

In Jacob's case, he loved Joseph more than his older brothers and demonstrated this favoritism openly and in a dramatic fashion. In no way did Jacob try to hide his partiality. The later part of verse three says, "...Also he made him a tunic of many colors." this term "tunic of many colors" is variously translated as "many-colored or richly ornamented." Still, the Hebrew word describes it as a robe extending to the ankles and the wrists, perhaps with an embroidered narrow stripe of color around the edge. It was a garment worn by the nobility and the wealthy. Joseph's brothers wore garments that were short and sleeveless. Joseph's brothers wade through swampy areas and carried sheep on their shoulders. Joseph's robe declared that he was exempt from manual labor and hardship. Even the light color of his robe indicated that he did not expect to get dirty or have it soiled from hard work. Whatever harmless intention Jacob had in expressing his love for Joseph, he, like many parents, failed to anticipate how others may perceive it in the family. Love considers the needs of others, and though Joseph held a special place in his father's heart, it proved to be too heavy of a burden for his immature sons to understand.

The good news is that generational curses can be stopped today. There are two basic principles to keep in mind:

1. A generational curse can come through the bloodline but broken through new choices and living patterns. This is the reason God gave Abraham one condition before giving him a covenant of blessing. *"The Lord had said to Abram, "Leave your native country, your relatives, and your father's family, and go to the land that I will show you. I will make you into a great nation. I will bless you and make you famous, and you will be a blessing to others"* (Genesis 12:1-2 NLT).

2. A generational curse can only be canceled by blood. *"In fact, according to the law of Moses, nearly everything was purified with blood. For without the shedding of blood, there is no forgiveness"* (Hebrews 9:22 NLT). We have been redeemed by the blood of Jesus Christ. Through faith and obedience in Christ, his blood washes us from all sins, because he became a curse for us so that we may have an abundant life.

Breaking Generational Curses

Recognize The Curse

First, one must admit to having a problem if they are to be set free and stay free. That sounds simple, but we live in a day and age of denial. No matter what has happened to us, we are responsible for our choices and decisions. If you want to be free, you must accept that it all comes down to what decisions you make today. As a king, no one had more reason to be protective of his public image than David. However, despite his personal mistakes and family history, nothing prevented his repentance.

> *"Have mercy upon me, O God, according to thy lovingkindness: according unto the multitude of thy tender mercies blot out my transgressions. Wash me thoroughly from mine iniquity, and cleanse me from my sin. For I acknowledge my transgressions: and my sin is ever before me. Against thee, thee only, have I sinned, and done this evil in thy sight: that thou mightest be justified when thou speakest, and be clear when thou judgest. Behold, I was shapen in iniquity; and in sin did my mother conceive me. Behold, thou desirest truth in the inward parts: and in the hidden part thou shalt make me to know wisdom"* (Psalms 51:1-6 KJV).

Break The Curse

As we apply God's Word and power to our lives and choose to walk in righteousness and obedience to God, the chains of bondage will be broken. James 1:25 says, *"But whoso looketh into the perfect law of liberty, and continueth therein, he being not a forgetful hearer, but a doer of the work, this man shall be blessed in his deed."* In breaking generational curses, give attention to these three things.

1. Give your life to Jesus; the blood of Jesus removes our sins. *"Therefore if any man be in Christ, he is a new creature: old things are passed away; behold, all things are become new"* (2 Corinthians 5:17 KJV). Despite how long your struggle has been before or since you've come to Christ, let this word increase your faith: without faith, we can go no further. How does Christ make all things new, you may ask. First, by re-purchasing you and making void any claim a curse may have on you. That is what it means to be redeemed; it is to be repurchased. *"Christ hath redeemed us from the curse of the law, being made a curse for us: for it is written, Cursed is every one that hangeth on a tree..."* (Galatian 3:13 KJV)

2. Fight the battle with spiritual weapons. Meet each day, fully covered and armed to withstand the enemy's advances.

The primary place for this battlefield is your mind. One must change one's mind before anyone can change one's health, location, or situation.

"Put on the whole armour of God, that ye may be able to stand against the wiles of the devil. For we wrestle not

> *One must first change one's mind before anyone can change their health, location, or situation.*

against flesh and blood, but against principalities, against powers, against the rulers of the darkness of this world, against spiritual wickedness in high places. Wherefore take unto you the whole armour of God, that ye may be able to withstand in the evil day, and having done all, to stand. Stand therefore, having your loins girt about with truth, and having on the breastplate of righteousness; And your feet shod with the preparation of the gospel of peace; Above all, taking the shield of faith, wherewith ye shall be able to quench all the fiery darts of the wicked. And take the helmet of salvation, and the sword of the Spirit, which is the word of God: Praying always with all prayer and supplication in the Spirit, and watching thereunto with all perseverance and supplication for all saints...." Ephesians 6:11-18 (KJV)

3. Regain control of your will. Romans chapter eight describes the victory we experience through the power of God and that it is the power of God that enables us to walk in

freedom. When Jesus shed His blood, he gave us the ability to be called sons of God. Those who are led by the Spirit of God are the sons of God. Through the Holy Ghost, God empowers us to live free from the torrents of temptations and the emotional triggers of our past. By the grace of God, we stand sober in mind with peace in our hearts, knowing that through the blood of Jesus, we can say no to these curses.

> "For God has not given us a spirit of fear and timidity, but of power, love, and self-discipline." (2 Timothy 1:7 NLT emphasis added)

Be encouraged, my friend, God is with you and for you. There is no reason to draw back; you must only believe, and his promises are yours.

Chapter 6

Music

Blessed is the people that know the joyful sound: they shall walk, O Lord, in the light of thy countenance. In thy name shall they rejoice all the day: and in thy righteousness shall they be exalted. *(Psalm 89:15-16 KJV)*

***

Music is a powerful tool by which spirits can transfer. The modern English word for 'music' is derived from Ancient Greek, "mousiké," an (art) to mean "of the Muses'" from which the word "muse" (to think) is derived. Music can influence and, in some cases, control the way a person thinks. Scripture is full of such examples, none more explicit than Ephesians 5:19. In Ephesians 5, Paul challenges the believers by describing how their life in Christ is built up and maintained. He emphasizes the importance of endurance and teaches how music can strengthen us. In verse 19, we see how music is used to help one keep the right mindset.

> "singing psalms and hymns and spiritual songs among yourselves, and making music to the Lord in your hearts." (Ephesians 5:19 NLT)

Music, by definition, is the art or science of composing or performing music or producing a sound perceived as pleasingly harmonious. Anyone who can make a sound (especially lyrics/words) pleasingly melodic can also make them pleasing or imperceptibly received. We use music when teaching young children their alphabet or multiplication tables. Where there is rhythm, there is repetition, and "repetition is the mother of mastery ." A typical response I get to this warning is, "I don't listen to the lyrics; I just like the beat." Give your brain more credit than that. Many scientific studies have proven that our brains store every experience as a memory. Though we may not be able to actively recall everything we hear, whatever we consume is ingested by the soul (mind). In Luke 8, Jesus taught on the seed and the sower, how a minor suggestion or (seed) could grow several times in the fruit (effect) it produces. He continued to warn them in Luke

Though we may not be able to actively recall everything we hear, whatever we consume is ingested by the soul

8:18 that they should be careful about *"how"* they hear, not just what they hear.

This call of caution is not for young people alone. Without a doubt, every secular genre has its degree of deceptive rebellion against the ways of God, but to be fair, "secular music" never claimed to be anything other than "secular" (without God). It's easy to think of genres like Heavy Metal, Pop, Rap, or R&B to guard against spiritual influences. In my experience, wickedly conceived songs are not exclusively reserved for the secular! Some of the most celebrated inspirational and gospel artists have produced morally ambiguous music that cultivates the worship of self to the point of invocating demons and the worship of Satan. If this sounds shocking, it's only a credit to how subtle the enemy's tactics are.

> 1 Timothy 4:1 says, *"Now the Spirit speaketh expressly, that in the latter times some shall <u>depart from the faith</u>, giving heed to <u>seducing spirits</u>, and doctrines of devils."* (KJV emphasis added)

For someone to "depart from the faith," they must first be in it. The potential damage of those with godly influence is so significant. Those of us within the body of Christ must cover one another in prayer, especially those in leadership positions who serve in administering the word and song. Anyone can start well, but it takes the grace of God to keep us from deviating ever so slightly but continuously into error. The Apostle Paul keeps us on guard by the charge he gave the believers in Galatians 5:7 (KJV); "Ye did run well; who did hinder you that ye should not obey the truth?"

Seducing spirits employ tactics that are superficially pleasant, subtle, or seemingly non-threatening. There is always a "who" behind what you're fighting through in spiritual warfare and breakthrough. Seducing spirits employ superficially pleasant, subtle, or seemingly non-threatening tactics. This alone shows the potential that music has to cause significant effects. Sometimes, these effects are evident long after initial exposure, and the damage is done. Music is "a sound perceived as pleasing." To be accurate, what may be considered "music" to some may not be "music" to others. For instance, every generation will declare jokingly that the music of "their day" is "real music," while everything on the radio nowadays is just noise. Allow me to emphasize a truth that every music label executive understands. Every generation has a "sound." 1 John 2:16 speaks of the lust of the flesh, the lust of the eye, and the pride of life, but we must understand that the enemy's use of these vices varies greatly and is very broad. Satan would much rather condemn us by fraud than by force. After all, it is more economical for him to pave the broad road to hell with comforts and compliments than marshall his demons in direct conflict to conquer your soul.

Everyone should seek to discern the intent behind the music we listen to, but perhaps doubly so for those with the gift of music. Again, we are confronted with the age-old warning to those with a brilliant beginning not to suffer an end marked by tragic failure. There is no more excellent portrait of falling from grace than the one who was first to do it (Luke 10:18). The Bible describes Lucifer as one of the most beautiful and uniquely gifted of all created beings. You may have heard him regarded as the first worship leader.

The idea of Satan as a master musician comes from Ezekiel 28:13. The New King James Version of the Bible (NKJV), speaking of Satan, says, "The workmanship of your timbrels and pipes was prepared for you on the day you were created." One thing is sure; his former station sat at the very center of worship, with all of the privileges of access it provides (Ezekiel 28:14).

> *"You were the anointed cherub who covers; I estab-*
> *lished you; You were on the holy mountain of God;*

You walked back and forth in the midst of fiery stones." (Ezekiel 28:14 NKJV)

Using Ezekiel 28:14 as a parallel, I urge worship leaders to take great care not to be deceived. Satan has a particular affinity for how he attacks worship leaders. Being a fallen worship leader, he understands a musician's susceptibility to pride. After all, it was pride that caused satan's fall. Ezekiel 28:17 NKJV says, *"Your heart was filled with pride because of all your beauty. Your wisdom was corrupted for the sake of your splendor. So I threw you to the ground and exposed you to the curious gaze of kings."*

Created with the beauty and ability none of his peers possessed, who couldn't imagine a created being so gifted would become so full of himself as to think he could overthrow God? To this day, satan still works to direct worship in any and every direction away from God the Father. While at a lesser scale, worship leaders are vulnerable to a similar error. Wielding the ability to set worship atmospheres by driving out evil spirits (1 Samuel 14:23), ushering in the presence of God (Psalms 100), and lifting burdens of heaviness (Isaiah 61:3), week after week, one can quickly lose sight of who is genuinely doing the work and worthy of the praise. Amid the amplified voices under their direction and the immediate crowd reactions to catchy song intros and crescendos, it can become intoxicating to be showered with adulations, compliments, and praise from congregants from week to week. After all, a minister of music walks *"back and forth amid fiery stones"*!

Walking Amongst Fiery Stones

Seldom do I see a musician dedicate his gift and time to one church. I know many who play for multiple churches and pastors within a given year. Most play for more than one church on a Sunday! To do this effectively is to provide an incredible service, one I consider an exception to the rule instead of the common practice it has become. Just as preachers of the word are developed and trained, it takes more than the delivery of a polished gift to make a preacher fit to travel and minister beyond their home flock. The high demand for musicians, however, has reduced the music ministry's entry requirement down to proficiency in performance.

> Ezekiel 28:15-16 NKJV: "You were blameless in all you did from the day you were created until the day evil was found in you. Your rich commerce led you to violence, and you sinned. So I banished you in disgrace from the mountain of

God. I expelled you, O mighty guardian, from your place among the stones of fire.

Those I pastor hear me often say, "Be careful who you hang around!" 1 Corinthians 15:33 warns that filthy communication corrupts good character. Notice in Ezekiel 28:15 that Lucifer started blameless from the day he was created, but verse 16 (NIV) shows that after his "widespread trade," he was then "filled with violence" before he sinned. Remember, there is always a "WHO" that stops you from running well (faithfulness). Over the years, I have witnessed times when God signals to the pastor his desire for a "fresh move."

Sometimes, the change God calls for requires a shift in music administration. What's interesting to me is the repetitious results that follow. Ideally, someone with the gift of music should be raised and trained out from the congregation. Nowadays, a recommendation is sought after by an external ministry partner to help identify a musician who shares the pastor's convictions. Sometimes, a musician is brought in from out of town with no local ties or connections. Within three months, the new musician is oddly connected and collaborating with an incumbent regime of musicians in that area. Eventually, these new relationships take a toll, and the new musician begins adopting a similar mindset different than that of the house they currently serve. Through their communication *(much trading)* with different people, the new musician is filled with another conviction, one that is contrary to the purpose for which they were initially aligned.

Whether subtlely or blatantly, a critical spirit arises, putting enmity between that pastor and the minister of music, causing the two to become at odds through a half-conscious cloud of miscommunication and misunderstandings. Within six months, "God's new musician" soon mirrors the attitudes and habits of the old regime. Once again stalling the change for which God was calling. Manifestations of this deception are a type of "pride of life." Romans 12:3 admonishes that no man should think more highly of themselves than they ought. Intoxicated by his splendor and skill, Lucifer sought to take on a role for which he was not created. In his heart, he asserted his will against the Father's Will four times (Isaiah 14:13-14). I have seen the same assertions in the hearts of musicians I have counseled. In the midst of their ministry frustrations (some of which are valid), some have admitted to feeling that they were in some ways more spiritual or had better insight into some matters than the pastors they supported. Though every circumstance differs, the principle remains: we serve a God of order. Never once did God violate his word to validate a gift.

Sure, there have been plenty of examples of God raising great shepherds out of the choir room. However, the choir isn't all that qualifies you for the congregation. God alone chooses our destiny and the work that our gifts will accomplish (Ephesians 2:9-10).

Equally discouraging is to see talented worship leaders leave the church altogether to

The choir does not qualify you for the congregation. God chooses our destiny and what our gifts will accomplish.

follow careers in the secular space. Very few start with this intention, but many roads also end here. I'm not saying that such artists are evil; however, there is much to say about the allure of personal glory and fame that pull on excellent musicians. Jesus describes these as those receiving the word, but *"...the cares of this world, and the deceitfulness of riches, and the lusts of other things entering in, choke the word, and it becometh unfruitful"* (Mark 4:19 KJV). I pray for our musicians who fight to keep their vow to the Lord; the temptations they face inwardly and outwardly are enough to sway the most anointed cherub.

Behind The Music

The book of James gives us a targeted template of temptation and its effect on us. The progression sin causes is the same despite the means or method used. While we are on music, let's apply his guiding principles to how we discern the activity of spirits and demonic oppression. For this exercise, let's look at the amplified Bible.

Know Yourself

> *"What leads to [the unending] quarrels and conflicts among you? Do they not come from your [hedonistic] desires that wage war in your [bodily] members [fighting for control over you]?"* (James 4:1 AMP)

James is straightforward and is known for his use of practical wisdom. Let us be sure to apply that wisdom here. Before you are inclined to call anything demonic, first check your desires and disciplines. Our base desires: food, shelter, sex, and security are natural and good when kept in their proper place. Should any spillover out of control, they quickly become fertile ground for spirits such as incontinence, covetousness (idolatry), lust, and fear (2 Timothy 3:2-4) to gain footholes. We have to know ourselves and be honest about what drives us. Who you are and what you desire affects the filter through which you perceive things and will significantly inform your life choices, great or small, be it a spouse or a song selection.

The Psalmist understood how vital self-awareness is to personal victory in Psalm 18:23, saying, *"I was also upright before him, and I kept myself from mine iniquity."* (KJV emphasis added)

Since we are talking about music in this chapter, we must point out how we have music for every mood. There is "love-making music" for couples, "hype music" for athletes, "driving music" for long trips, sad music for melancholy moments, and elevator music for waiting; the list goes on. To be sure, music is as varied as the human experience. The Spirit must lead us and not our changing moods. Indulging in music that reflects our attitude can be dangerous. For example, a fleeting thought can become an album-long fight with temptation or depression. That's why the Psalmist in scripture maintained the habit of talking to himself, taking responsibility for the posture of his soul (mind) by dictating the song he should sing. "Why art thou cast down, O my soul? and why art thou disquieted within me? hope in God: for I shall yet praise him, who is the health of my countenance, and my God" (Psalms 43:5 KJV). James 4 challenges us to look inward, where our battles begin.

Understand Where Error Comes From

"This [superficial] wisdom is not that which comes down from above, but is earthly (secular), natural (unspiritual), even demonic." (James 3:15 AMP emphasis added)

James shows how tempta-tion has a "progression" to it. It begins centering on the "earth-ly" need of our base desires.

It is easy for Soul(ish) music to gain popularity quickly; the key to its appeal is that it emphasizes personal desires over the priority of God's will.

When our needs are inflamed, our capacity for deception grows, aided by our "natural (unspiritual) mind." The King James version translates natural as "sensual," better known as "the flesh." Not the flesh and blood that make up our bodies, but rather the "fleshly mind" (way of thinking) described in Romans 8:7, which is "hostile toward God." It is with the mind (soul) that music is expressed and experienced. The renewed mind led by the Spirit of God can sing "spiritual songs," as mentioned in Ephesians 5:19. However, the unre-generate mind is at odds with God by default. It can not think of things above, only those beneath, tangible, visible, and immediate. Have you ever heard a sermon or read a book that seemed only to emphasize the "here and now"? The entire subject of concern emphasizes our attention on the visible and immediate. Such messages do not come from the Spirit but from the soul. I point this out to invite you to carefully consider some of the "gospel music" you enjoy. Some gospel songs have omitted the mention of Jesus and are so generic in their themes that they are played and performed on every media platform. Soul(ish) music can be beautiful, masterfully composed, and incredibly relatable, but it doesn't glorify God. Instead, it emphasizes self-expression and personal fulfillment. Gospel music should carry the gospel, inspired by the Spirit, but this is not always done. It is easy for Soul(ish) music to gain popularity quickly; the key to its appeal is that it emphasizes personal desires over the priority of God's will.

A Shepard's Ear

I was trained by the best. I had the incredible privilege of serving the late Apostle C.L. Long as his assistant pastor for 25 years. The entire time, I was being groomed for where I now stand. Looking back, I recall moments of training that I then didn't recognize. My father was somewhat unconventional. My father sometimes saw things the rest of us were unaware of. Like the young man in 2 Kings 6, my pastor had to pray to God to open my eyes a time or two. Presumptuously young, I would privately contest my father's perspective on matters I felt strongly about. Being the patient father he was, he sometimes let me finish my point. Then replied, "You'll understand when you're the pastor." All debate at that point was over, but he later elaborated that there is something "different" that God gives Pastors (Jeremiah 3:15) to enable them to lead a flock. Like any good shepherd, you must know your congregation in Spirit and ability.

If you are a Pastor, you are the first praiser, worshiper, and disciple of Jesus Christ for your church.

If you are a Pastor, you are the first praiser, worshiper, and disciple of Jesus Christ for your church. When God visits your service, you ought to be the first person to welcome him in. If the enemy seeks to attack your people, you are the first to take authority, and when worship becomes misguided, you are the first to initiate course correction.

Be involved and partner with your Musical Director. Provide your input on song selection, and make sure you are clear on the lyrics, and they are clear on your vision. Challenge those in your music ministry to provide new recommendations for music to be submitted for review. Meet with your choirs and praise team members, and make an effort for them to hear your heart while at the same time listening closely to theirs. Doing so will help you better understand their concerns and needs. Make sure that those who are faithful are getting their proper rest and have the opportunity to be ministered to as well. As much as their gift may help you, we owe it to every member to minister to their whole man. Even if that means having a service or two without their gift. A soul can grow cold while singing the hottest new songs.

Psalm 89:15 says, *"Blessed is the people that know the joyful sound: they shall walk, O Lord, in the light of thy countenance."* You must remain sensitive to ensure your house produces "the proper sound." Those who worship God can only do so in Spirit and truth (John 4:24). It is possible to play all the right notes and sing every word correctly while holding the right key (truth), all while harboring the wrong Spirit! As pastors, we must know the "sound"; satan is the king of counterfeits (2 Thessalonians 2:9). We must stand at the gate to make sure the enemy gains no ground by way of a wounded heart, proud looks, or haughty spirits that aim to turn God's worship into idol worship.

> **A soul can grow cold while singing the hottest new songs.**

Moses Discerns The Sound of Idol Worship

*"Now when Joshua heard the noise of the peo-
ple as they shouted, he said to Moses, "There is a
sound of battle in the camp." But Moses said, "It
is not the sound of the cry of victory, Nor is it the
sound of the cry of defeat; But I hear the sound of
singing." And as soon as he approached the camp
and he saw the calf and the dancing, Moses' anger
burned; and he threw the tablets from his hands
and smashed them at the foot of the mountain."
(Exodus 32:17-19 AMP)*

In no way do I condone a pastor losing their cool like
this. It does reiterate how God's servant must have a zeal for
God and the things of God. Good worship is not defined by
having good music, dancing for joy, or deep tears. Worship
only exists when God is at the center of it all. Worship occurs
when we set aside everything: our blessings, our struggles, and
our petitions. Any worship that isn't centered on Christ is a
golden calf.

Chapter 7

Indulgence: Food,
Pharmacy & Desire

---

*"What? know ye not that your body is the temple of the
Holy Ghost which is in you, which ye have of God, and
ye are not your own? For ye are bought with a price:
therefore glorify God in your body, and in your spirit,
which are God's."*

(1 Corinthians 6:19-20 KJV)

***

In the preceding verses of 1 Corinthians 6, the Apostle
Paul challenges believers in spiritual maturity. First, their
ability to overlook an offense, and second, their capacity to
exercise restraint. Just because you can, Paul argues, doesn't
make it profitable (1 Corinthians 6: 12). Paul says, *"All things*

are lawful for me, but I will not be brought under the power of any." Addiction can come from many things, and by it, many fall and find it hard to rise. Food is no exception, and for many God-loving people, it stands as the "vice of choice."

Food

As we've discussed previously, the Bible warns that in the last days, *men will be lovers of pleasures rather than lovers of God* (2 Tim 3:2-4). Though the days of King Nebuchadnezzar and his golden statue have passed, we are still bombarded by a daily beckoning to bow to the world's idolatry. It may seem foreign to picture this through modern lenses, but anything that turns our love for God to any other focus is idolatry. When sensuality takes over a person's life, their worship becomes worthless because their focus is no longer on God but on the affairs of men. 1 Timothy 5:6 says, *"But the widow [person] who lives for pleasure is dead even while she lives"* (emphasis added).

The scriptures show examples of God's displeasure for sensuality/carnality. In my experience, many Christians would disqualify themselves from this category, thinking it only pertains to unbridled sexual desires or lude-ness. Simply put, carnality is the preoccupation with earthly matters. Along the way, we forget that we are not of this world, and instead, we work to make our place in the world while the world makes its place in our hearts.

They aren't busy in ministry, but busybodies, stirring up discontent, and are more concerned about having fun than kingdom fellowship.

God can not use a carnal man. A carnal man can not understand God's word or receive his leadership. The "carnal man" counts spiritual things as foolishness (1 Corinthians 2:14). Esau fell out of favor with God due to this aspect of his character. Esau preferred a bowl of porridge over becoming a prince among men (Romans 9:13, Hebrews 12:17). A carnal Christian is like the lukewarm church, as seen in Revelation 3:15-16, which God vomits up. As a pastor, I marvel at times at what motivates people. I often tease at the thought of calling an all-night prayer service and being able to count on both hands the members who will most likely show up without complaint. But If we were to put on one of our famous Crab Feasts dinners, we would have a line wrapped around the parking lot.

Even my group leaders know to bring snacks sometimes to their meetings. It helps take the edge off the hungry complainers who look for reasons why ideas don't work. These types of members concern me greatly. They no longer come to serve but to socialize, and ministry talk only gets in the way of their agenda. They aren't busy in ministry but busybodies, stirring up discontent, and are more concerned about having fun than kingdom fellowship. In Philippians 3:18-19 (KJV), Paul deals with such ones in his day. He said, *"For many walk, of whom I have told you often, and now tell you even weeping, that they are the enemies of the cross of Christ: Whose end is destruction, whose God is their belly, and whose glory is in their shame, who mind earthly things."*

"Dear friend, I pray that you may enjoy good health and that all may go well with you, even as your soul is getting along well" (3 John 2 NIV). As we grow spiritually, the Holy Spirit leads and guides us into all truth, practical and supernatural. As discussed throughout the book, we want to be aware of the entry points the enemy uses to derail us. Food and drink are other examples of how a good thing can be turned into an evil device, making us susceptible to sickness, poverty, death, and spiritual dullness.

"For this cause, there are weak and sickly among you, and many sleep"

I preached a sermon in 2022 entitled The Meaning of Communion. In it, we examined Paul's address to the Corinthians regarding their behavior during the Lord's feast. 1 Corinthians 11:23-25, Paul recounts the inaugural purpose and intention of the Lord's Supper, showing how it served as a memorial of our Lord's sacrifice, empowering us to reflect on how our lives should qualitatively reflect Christ's sacrifice to bring God glory. By this time, the tradition had been corrupted from a love feast to a convention of carnality. In verses 17-22, some of the Corinthian believers treated fellowship as a means to show off earthly goods instead of doing good to others. They lost the spirit of unity due to their worldly cliques and class statuses. The church became like any other place where the poor were reminded that they were of lesser degree, and the rich were further blinded to their genuine need of the savior.

While we love everyone, communion is for "Believers Only." There is no other way to "worthily" take part in it.

Context is everything! Paul explained that their participation in this feast meant more than passing bread and drinking wine for a good time. In 1 Corinthians 11:26-27 (KJV), Paul says, *"For as often as ye eat this bread, and drink this cup, ye do shew the Lord's death till he come. Wherefore whosoever shall eat this bread, and drink this cup of the Lord, unworthily, shall be guilty of the body and blood of the Lord."* To "unworthily" eat the bread and drink the cup means to do so for *any purpose other than its created intent.* So what does that mean for us? Like many others, my church observes communion with a tiny precut cracker and a sip of wine, but Paul's warning is as applicable to us today as it was to the Corinthian saints. In the sermon, believers are encouraged not to take communion for granted. While we love everyone, communion is for "Believers Only." There is no other way to "worthily" take part in it.

"But let a man examine himself, and so let him eat of that bread, and drink of that cup" (1 Corinthians 11:28). I remember growing up as a boy in the '70-'80s, and it seemed to me that there was a broader understanding of the fear of the Lord than what is practiced today. Conviction of sin was preached regularly with much effectiveness, not just in my church but overall. So much so that I can remember a time when my friends would try and skip communion services if they had done something "especially" wrong. We understood what it meant to take communion "unworthily." What I see more common today is what my friends also failed to understand about "self-examination."

Christ died for the ungodly, and the Bible teaches us that he who says that he has no sin makes God a liar, and his word is not in us (1 John 1:10). So as I minister today, I encourage the church to, *run to the table, not from it.* I only ask that you wash your hands! The tone of my communion services typically resembles James 4:8-10; *"Draw nigh to God, and he will draw nigh to you. Cleanse your hands, ye sinners; and purify your hearts, ye double minded. Be afflicted, and mourn, and weep: let your laughter be turned to mourning, and your joy to heaviness. Humble yourselves in the sight of the Lord, and he shall lift you up"*. I truly believe that we can be healed, set free, and delivered at the table. Still, just as 1 Corinthians 11 shows, carnality will contaminate any holy endeavor if the "old man" is not crucified.

Unlike the first-century church, our communion custom today makes it impossible

"run to the table, not from it." I only ask that you wash your hands!

for anyone to flaunt status with food. Yet pride in titles and positions makes sharing the same alter-call for repentance difficult. A proud heart is perhaps more dangerous than the state of the Corinthian church in chapter 11. Their crimes were outward and evident while the enemy battles us at the alters of our hearts where no one can see except God and us. Lack of transparency complicates things for those needing spiritual reinforcement but are too embarrassed to come boldly in their time of need. So, we approach the table with dirty hands to appear as if we are okay; even worse, we "go through the motions" so our leader or Pastor doesn't ask why we've missed church. Brothers and sisters, this is not what communion is about; to participate in this way, or for any other reason, is to do so unworthily. Carnality would have us go through life making "Esau deals," where we'd prefer "feeling good" for the moment at the cost of our eternal future.

Moving on from communion, the fundamental correlation it draws between food and fellowship is consistent through scripture. Thinking back on the many things my father taught me over the years, I remember him saying, *"Be careful who you have dinner with; before you know it, they'll know all of your business."* Keeping good company is more than keeping secrets; it's about maintaining good character (1 Cor 15:33). Spiritual warfare has taught me over the years that it's a battle fought in the mind. The enemy also fights how we think as we navigate relationships with people and places that claim to be kin to us.

Relationships

Carnality would have us go through life making "Esau deals," where we'd prefer "feeling good" for the moment at the cost of our eternal future.

Social connections are relationships where we share degrees of community, family ties, or religious associations. These areas especially ought to be diligently discerned and decisively handled. In 1 Corinthians 5:11 (NLT), Paul says, *"I meant that you are not to associate with anyone who claims to be a believer yet indulges in sexual sin, or is greedy, or worships idols, or is abusive, or is a drunkard, or cheats people. Don't even eat with such people."* Even now, reading this scripture, I can hear some of you saying, "That's old school," and you'd be right. Paul was building on the fundamentals of Proverbs 22:24-25 (NLT): *Don't befriend angry people or associate with hot-tempered people, or you will learn to be like them and endanger your soul.*

Associations are powerful in facilitating the exchange of ideas and establishing commitments. Jesus was no less definitive in his ability to draw the line when someone tried to use family status to supersede his spiritual purpose. While ministering and teaching, someone came to Jesus, informing him that his mother and brother were outside, desiring to speak to him. Matthew 12:48-50 (KJV) says, *"But he answered and said unto him that told him, Who is my mother? and who are my brethren? And he stretched forth his hand toward his disciples, and said, Behold my mother and my brethren! For whosoever shall do the will of my Father which is in heaven, the same is my brother, and sister, and mother."*

Critics and skeptics had called Jesus many things, but a religious zealot was not one of them. Singularly driven to complete The Father's work, Jesus kept people and things in their proper place. Jesus was not without natural affection; he cared for his mother deeply and attended to her care until his last breath (John 19:26-27). However, Jesus demonstrates strict and decisive discernment when prioritizing kingdom business from personal business. Like Jesus, we, too, must refuse to allow the squeeze of social convention to compromise our convictions. Because of this stance, you may find yourself an outcast, the butt of a joke or two, or perhaps regarded at times as being "religious over much" by fellow believers. Be encouraged, *"Blessed are you when they revile and persecute you and say all kinds of evil against you falsely for My sake. Rejoice and be exceedingly glad, for great is your reward in heaven, for so they persecuted the prophets who were before you. You are the salt of the earth; but if the salt loses its flavor, how shall it be seasoned? It is then good for nothing but to be thrown out and trampled underfoot by men"* (Matthew 5:11-13 NKJV).

> *Like Jesus, we, too, must refuse to allow the squeeze of social convention to compromise our convictions.*

There is a powerful transference of spirits through food, drink, and alcohol. Through these avenues, spirits can be transferred negatively or positively. Perhaps the most positive is the sacred act of communion when done correctly. However, we can intentionally or inadvertently commune with spirits that are not of God (Revelation 2:14) when the desire for pleasure drives us and when worship is fueled by self-will. For example, in 1 Corinthians 10:19-22, Paul admonishes the believers at Corinth that they can no longer keep some of their old social functions or patronize invitations to traditional feasts of the culture. Upon Paul's first arrival in Greece, he addressed the hearers on Mars Hill, citing their culture as very religious because they worship many things (Acts 17:22-34). Perhaps remembering Isaiah's words, Paul exercised extraordinary patience, recalling the scripture, *"All of us, like sheep, have strayed away. We have left God's paths to follow our own. Yet the LORD laid on him [Christ] the sins of us all"* (Isaiah 53:6 NLT). For every temple in Corinth, a cult group led and facilitated the activity of worship dedicated to the acclaimed deity it was named after. The Latin root word "cult" is where the term originates to mean cultivated/worship.

Paul revealed to the Corinthian believers that these temples were not dedicated to any deity but to demons, for there is only one true God. So, while there is nothing inherently wrong with meats, grains, or vegetables in and of themselves, eating food prepared as part of accursed rituals or activities paves the way for unholy alignment with evil spirits. I can almost hear Paul through the scriptures, counseling the spiritually immature as I have done for years. They argue and assure me they are strong enough to attend the club, meeting, or cookout. They claim they can be a witness and not be affected by other things. Trust me; I've heard them all. Those who use such arguments are not being logical or spiritual; their appeal is almost always more sentimental, looking for a loophole to straddle the fence of technicalities to keep old friends. I understand the desire to support a friend and enjoy great-tasting food while being a witness in a dark place. As impressive as that may sound, it doesn't work that way. 1 Corinthians 10:21-22 (NLT) Paul says, *"You cannot drink from the cup of the Lord and from the cup of demons, too. You cannot eat at the Lord's Table and at the table of demons, too. What? Do we dare to rouse the Lord's jealousy? Do you think we are stronger than he is?"* I'm with Paul on this: don't tempt the Lord, and don't fool yourself into believing that you somehow have greater spiritual strength than anyone else. We pray to be led away from temptations, not to fall headlong into them. As music is to the ear, so are pleasures to our flesh; whatever our bodies do affects our souls.

Desires

The spiritually mature have learned over the years what it means to make special restrictions on personal pleasures for the sake of their calling. These restrictions are called convictions; they are private and usually more restrictive than the general command scripture provides for holy living. For example, the dietary restriction for Samson and Jesus Christ as Nazerits (Numbers 6:1-8) did not violate Jewish law. In many ways, denoting their consecration to the Lord for a specific task was more stringent. As explained in Romans Chapter 14, I have no opinion about what you *should* eat, only *how we eat*. All that we do or don't do must be to the glory of God. There is no need for fruitless debate in *your choice of food*, for this falls under the category of conviction, which is specific to every person but should be evident in bringing glory to God through the person's health and fitness to serve. Psalm 25:12-14 (KJV) says, *"What man is he that feareth the Lord? Him shall he teach in the way that he shall choose. His soul shall dwell at ease; and his seed shall inherit the earth. The secret of the Lord is with them that fear him; and he will shew them his covenant"* (emphasis added).

The spiritually mature have learned over the years what it means to make special restrictions on personal pleasures for the sake of their calling.

I am not one to contest what the Lord may have told an individual; we'll let time be the judge in that case. However, as my ministerial board will attest, I only have one rule: preach the gospel. Preaching convictions, however, is scripturally forbidden; doing so can easily foster disputes, and create factions as it edifies no one and binds people to instructions God intended only the preacher to follow. Many world religions practice specific disciplines, such as prayer, fasting, and restrictive diets. Colossians 2:23 (NLT) says, *"These rules may seem wise because they require strong devotion, pious self-denial, and severe bodily discipline. But they provide no help in conquering a person's evil desires."* Be on guard against the spirit of pride; the enemy will use any angle to maneuver you into error however he can. He will stoop so low as to use an unhealthy relationship with food to lead you astray. *"Now the Holy Spirit tells us clearly that in the last times some will turn away from the true faith; they will follow deceptive spirits and teachings that come from demons. These people are hypocrites and liars, and their consciences are dead. They will say it is wrong to be married and wrong to eat certain foods. But God created those foods to be eaten with thanks by faithful people who know the truth. Since everything God created is good, we should not reject any of it but receive it with thanks."*(1 Timothy 4:1-4 NLT)

Our desires, even noble ones, must be tempered by the Holy Spirit. Having religious zeal is profitable when it is according to the knowledge of God. On the other hand, half-hearted compliance by believers who go along to get along will never experience what it means to please God, because their behavior is not built on faith, but social convention. God looks at the heart, not just our behaviors. So be sure that you affirm in faith that which you say you believe. Romans 14:23 reminds us that, *"whatever is not done in faith, is sin."*

Unreformed Witches:

"Neither repented they of their murders, nor of their sorceries, nor of their fornication, nor of their thefts." (Revelation 9:21)

There is a healthy amount of inconvenient truth, which some believers, particularly new converts, find hard to hear. One of those truths is that the devil comes to church, too. We shouldn't find it odd that evil spirits are present, primarily when spiritual activity occurs. The danger lies in the inability to distinguish between good and evil. No one is born an expert. There have been times through the years when I had been convinced that a person, a plan, a car, or a business deal was the best thing for me. Time would later prove me wrong, leaving little to show for my optimism except for a few new bruises and sometimes a bill. The devil is intentional about making evil as imperceivable as possible. Solomon prayed, *"Give me an understanding heart so that I can govern your people well and know the difference between right and wrong.*

For who by himself is able to govern this great people of yours?" (1 Kings 3:9)

Every sincere Pastor would do well to pray Solomon's prayer. Leading a church con-

...danger lies in the inability to distinguish between good and evil.

gregation can be hazardous to the shepherd. My father had a way of reminding us of kingdom principles during ministry work. One of my favorites is; *"All Kinds in the net."* As fishers of men, we will encounter all kinds of people, some true, some false. It reminds me of a sermon my father preached many years ago entitled; "Snakes In The Pews." Witchcraft is nuanced, and there is more to it than what is popularized on television. The simplest definition of witchcraft is control, illegitimate control.

The sensual, fleshly person cannot worship; true worship must be done unto God in spirit and truth (John 4:24). God is sovereign and in control, but the witch would disagree. The appeal of religion to some is that they see it, or even God, as a *means* to get what they want in life. They think things will go their way if they say the right thing and connect with the right people. That's not coming to God to worship; that's coming to God to *control*. The Bible says that the sin of rebellion is the same as the spirit of witchcraft, and stubbornness is the same as iniquity and idolatry. This is important to call out because the same spirit can manifest its will in slightly different ways. The impact of scripture illuminates us to realize that we are not as far removed from the "biblical times" as some would suppose. Spirits are real, and spirits do not die. We need the Bible to help us see what they are by shining its light into the darkness, saving us from our stumbling.

Can a believer be an Unreformed Witch? When a person comes to God, remember they are coming from somewhere! In Acts 19, we read about Paul's ministry visit to Ephesus, where he ministered to Jews and Greeks. It came to the point where the "*name of the Lord Jesus spread abroad and was greatly honored*" (verse 17). After conviction set in, many came to saving faith in Jesus and repented: "*Many who became believers confessed their sinful practices. <u>A number of them who had been practicing sorcery</u> brought their incantation books and burned them at a public bonfire. The value of the books was several million dollars*" (Acts 19:18-19 NLT emphasis added). Dad was right, "All kinds in the net." People who have a propensity to a spirit of witchcraft have a driving desire to gain and maintain control over events and people. This kind of person will act to create their own desired outcome.

Pharmacy

Sorcery is sometimes used synonymously with witchcraft, but that's incorrect; sorcery is but one of many tools

People who have a proclivity to a spirit of witchcraft have a driving desire to gain and maintain control over events and people.

a person with a spirit of witchcraft would employ. A simple word search shows sorcery's relation to words like voodoo, divination, and medicine. That's right, medicine; in fact, the Greek root word for sorcery is pharmakeia, the word from which we derive the use of the word pharmacy. Sorcery is the practical use and manipulation of natural or synthesized ingredients meant to be ingested or applied directly to a person's body to change one's state or condition. This includes the act of altering food, drinks, or body ointments in such a way as to induce or influence sickness, addiction, intoxication, or infatuation: to put it in broader, more secular terms, medicine.

My mother had been a Pastor's wife for over 50 years and dealt with many of "those kinds in the net." I would be lying if I told you that every "baked cake" sent to my father's office was eaten. The dumpster mice may have enjoyed it, but my father never did. I remember a few years back, there were members of our church who seemed like reasonable, well-to-do people. Every once in a while, they would take trips down south to "see family." One day, my father received a heartfelt letter detailing what these people went down south to do. They were still active in the occult, and the "family" they supposedly visited was instead a merchant from whom they regularly bought "roots." Jesus said not everyone that says unto me, Lord, Lord, will enter the Kingdom of God. This is no marvel, for the devil knows how to disguise himself as an angel of light (2 Corinthians 11:14).

I know of a ministry friend who was not as restrictive in receiving food gifts from congregants. One day, that all changed as he and his family were given food purposely poisoned to kill him. He and a few immediate family members needed to be hospitalized, but by the grace of God, they survived. Since then, no one in his family has received so much as a mint from anyone during their ministry work. Sadly, such precautions must be taken, but Jesus was adamant when he said, "I send you as sheep among wolves." Ministry can be messy; we preach the gospel sometimes under hostile conditions, cultivating the best in people while fully aware of human depravity's depths.

So, can a believer be an unreformed witch? Simon was! We find Simon's story recorded in Acts 8. Philip the Evangelist was preaching the gospel in Samaria with great effectiveness and power. As Philip preached, the gospel spread fast and began winning over a crowd of people whom Simon once had *control*.

> *"But there was a certain man, called Simon, which beforetime in the same city used sorcery, and bewitched the people of Samaria, giving out that himself was some great one: To whom they all gave heed, from the least to the greatest, saying, This man is the great power of God. And to him they had regard, because that of long time he had bewitched them with sorceries." (Acts 8:9-11 KJV)*

Philip preached Jesus Christ, taught the people about the Kingdom of God, and Baptized them in the name of Jesus (Acts 8:12). The Bible declares that Simon also believed and followed Philip (Acts 8:13). If the Bible says he believed, then he believed. I will not debate or doubt Simon's sincerity, as it is for many Christians; sincerity is not the issue: sanctification is. Our repentance is only as strong as the distance we put between our old life habits and acting on God's word. Jesus taught that when an evil spirit (like witchcraft) is driven out of a man, he may enjoy a season of freedom before that spirit returns with a desire to reclaim its former dwelling place. Though a person may be swept clean of their old life, if they do not fill the void left by past behaviors, it becomes an idle entry point for the same or worse habit to fester and grow.

No different than any of us, the scripture shows Simon's weakness. He had a preoccupation with miracles, signs, and wonders. Acts 8:13 says, *"Then Simon himself believed also: and when he was baptized, he continued with Philip, and wondered, beholding the miracles and signs which were done."* We believe in miracles because we believe in God; Simon, however, *"wondered"* after them. Jesus taught that only a wicked and adulterous person *"looks"* for signs and wonders (Matthew 12:39). This remained in Simon's heart, but we don't see him openly bring this up with Philip, perhaps biding his time or not sure if the miracles he saw where unique only to Philip. After news spread about the Samarians coming to the faith, the apostles visited and prayed for them to receive the Holy Ghost.

"And when Simon saw that through laying on of the apos-

We believe in miracles because we believe in God...

tles' hands the Holy Ghost was given, he offered them money, Saying, Give me also this power, that on whomsoever I lay hands, he may receive the Holy Ghost. But Peter said unto him, Thy money perish with thee, because thou hast thought that the gift of God may be purchased with money. Thou hast neither part nor lot in this matter: for thy heart is not right in the sight of God. Repent therefore of this thy wickedness, and pray God, if perhaps the thought of thine heart may be forgiven thee. For I perceive that thou art in the gall of bitterness, and in the bond of iniquity. Then answered Simon, and said, Pray ye to the Lord for me, that none of these things which ye have spoken come upon me." (Acts 8:18-20 KJV)

Being a "former sorcerer," he understood the importance of spiritual power, but his heart was not right before God. Tempted by the lure of once again having power and popularity, the spirit of witchcraft found its opening to reclaim its old home. True to its character, the spirit of witchcraft seeks to control the things that only belong to God. He offered money to receive power. This was not sowing a seed of faith but offering a bribe. By the Holy Ghost, Peter perceived that he was now bound by the spirit of bitterness and addiction (bond of iniquity). His "bitterness" perhaps settled on him shortly after his conversion, realizing that his faith ended his livelihood. Only the Holy Spirit can empower us to walk in righteousness, and like many who are new to the ways of holiness, Simon perhaps felt the need to hide his unconquered sinful habits. We don't have to go further than Judas Iscariot to see how secret sins may not prevent you from performing your religious duties, but they leave the door ajar wide enough for satan to enter and occupy (John 12:6, John 13:27).

Keep an eye out for the "Simon's" you encounter. They may be enthusiastic and engaging on spiritual matters, with little fruit to show and even less accountability when their behavior is challenged. Their response is similar to Simon's reaction whenever such a person is rebuked. Like Simon, when challenged with scriptural standards, they say, "*Yall pray for me; the Lord is still working on me*" (Acts 8:24). The unreformed sorcerer would sooner stand in a public prayer line than sincerely repent. Ultimately fulfilling the final stage of Jesus' warning regarding those unreformed; "...and the last state of that man is worse than the first. Even so shall it be also unto this wicked generation" (Matthew 12:45).

God has given us a spirit of power, love, and self-control. We must discern what we eat,

Godly principles protect us from our desires, cravings, and the opinions of others.

who we eat from, and who we eat with. Setting boundaries of principle helps us do just that. Godly principles protect us from our desires, cravings, and the opinions of others. "A person without self-control is like a city with broken-down walls" (Proverbs 25:28 NLT).

Psychic Prayer

James 4:1-3 KJV says, "From whence come wars and fightings among you? come they not hence, even of your lusts that war in your members? Ye lust, and have not: ye kill, and desire to have, and cannot obtain: ye fight and war, yet ye have not, because ye ask not. Ye ask, and receive not, because ye ask amiss, that ye may consume it upon your lusts."

Some people attempt to influence God to cause someone or something to move in a particular manner. Whether knowingly or unknowingly, they fail to consider God's will for that person. Praying with the wrong motives causes others to act, think, and feel in a certain way. This sort of manipulation I call **Psychic Prayer**, or as James 3:15 describes it, is the prayer that is motivated by earthly, sensual, and demonic wisdom. "*Psychic Prayer*" is a form of witchcraft that is fundamentally demonic. James 3:15 KJV says, "*This wisdom descendeth not from above, but is earthly, **sensual**, devilish*" (emphasis added). The Greek origin for the word translated as sensual is the word psuché, which is defined as "breath, or the soul," used to express the presence of (b) the human soul, (c) the soul as the seat of affections and will, (d) the self, (e) a human person, an individual. Strong's Concordance 5590 shows that Psuché is where the root of the English words "psyche" and "psychology" – soul (psyche) is derived. Psychic Prayer occurs when a person, in essence, prays amiss, insisting on their intentions and desires instead of seeking God's will.

For instance, to pray about something you are so convinced you must have (such as a young man who desired a particular young lady), and if your mind is already made up as to the answer, your prayer becomes a form of manipulation to God for that person. You may believe you are to have that person, but you are deceiving yourself and allowing a *seducing spirit* to blind your eyes to the truth. For a person to put their "claim" on another is bringing one under the curse of spiritual bondage. The object of someone's desire in this way may not even be aware that this is happening, which can contribute to them experiencing unwarranted spiritual pressure.

The *spirit of lust,* for instance, can also be transmitted from person to person. For example, a young woman may wonder why she is suddenly physically attracted to a young man or oddly bombarded with sexual thoughts involving him when there have been no previous inclinations of natural attraction. If one cannot see through this, they may be unwittingly coerced into a relationship they would not have otherwise had. Such imposed "spiritual bondage" does not please God and is unhealthy for everyone involved.

The following statement is critical. *Psychic Prayer* also occurs when a group of people, perhaps a church auxiliary or

> *Psychic Prayer occurs when a person, in essence, prays amiss, insisting on their intentions and desires instead of seeking God's will.*

intercessory group, gathers for payer to make "intercession to God" for a person they "knowingly" are trying to force into a particular action or frame of mind. It can occur when a Pastor is expected to make a decisive choice, and the group wants to persuade him to take a particular position or make a decision that would be favorable to them. They may pray to God that he "sees our way of thinking" and that "his eyes may be opened" to see that their preferred way is the right way.

Consequences of Indulgence

- **Proverbs 21:17 ESV** - Poverty: Whoever loves pleasure will be a poor man; he who loves wine and oil will not be rich.

- **Proverbs 20:1 KJV** - Shame/Wrath: Wine is a mocker, strong drink is raging: and whosoever is deceived thereby is not wise.

- **Proverbs 23:21 ESV** - Addiction/Poverty: For the

drunkard and the glutton will come to poverty, and slumber will clothe them with rags.

- **Hosea 4:11 ESV** - Immorality/Spiritual Dullness: Whoredom, wine, and new wine, which take away the understanding.

Later, we will discuss demonic stronghold groupings, but it is important to note how scripture parallels seemingly opposite behaviors to a singular theme. For example, drunkenness and gluttony are regarded as equals, just as wine and strong drink are synonymous with one without self-control. Remember Jesus' parable about the servants and their talents? The servant who hid his talent in the ground was described as wicked and lazy (Matthew 25:26). God's wisdom enables us to rightly discern the spirit at work. However, it may manifest differently from person to person. The Spirit of truth looks past religious facades to deliver the saint who stress-eats the same way it delivers the drunkard from the bottle. How often are we tempted as leaders to openly rebuke wicked murmurers and complainers who frustrate our purpose while at the same time catering to what appears to be frail-hearted saints, only to find that the ones we coddle the most have no intention of being healed or getting involved? They're just wicked and lazy.

Chapter 8

Objects & Artifacts

Neither shalt thou bring an abomination into thine house, lest thou be a cursed thing like it: but thou shalt utterly detest it, and thou shalt utterly abhor it; for it is a cursed thing.

(Deuteronomy 7:26 KJV)

***

We must discern what we take in as food and what we take into our homes. Remember the definition and scope of sorcery we defined earlier. Sorcery and idolatry can extend beyond food to objects and materials worn or displayed. Many homes and people invite demonic influence with the presence of such things in their possession. These items can be as overt as shrines, occult symbols, ancient artifacts, healing/chakra crystals, ouija boards, and tarot cards.

Contrary to what some may consider the items mentioned above as "obvious evils," many sincere believers are taken in by seemingly benign things like earrings, necklaces, bracelets, rings, tainted articles of clothing, pieces of art, or molded figures. That which God forbids can also apply to objects such as contaminated candles, incense, perfumes, soups, and even counterfeit "holy water or handkerchiefs" propagated by false prophets and fetish priests.

Before we continue in this study, let me acknowledge the tension you may be feeling regarding God's tone. The enemy no doubt intimidates believers with the fear of appearing legalistic, prudish, or "religious over much" when scripture challenges us in areas of personal discipline for sanctification. You'll find this necessary, particularly in matters of deliverance and freedom, and why God uses such robust and decisive language, teaching us to strive to have "no gray areas" in our walk of faith. As Jesus cast out devils, his disciples were offended that others did the same, following Jesus' example. Jesus's response was unexpected, creating a famous quote often used out of its original context.

Let's look together:

Luke 9:49-50 KJV

And John answered and said, Master, we saw one casting out devils in thy name; and we forbad him, because he followeth not with us. And Jesus said unto him, *Forbid him not: for he that is not against us is for us.* (emphasis added)

See here, Jesus' quote is regarding the importance of one's alliance when engaged in spiritual warfare and deliverance. John stated that this other person casts out devils in Jesus' name. The implication is that this "other person" was doing so successfully; otherwise, this account would be closer to the unfortunate scenario involving the seven sons of Sceva (Acts 19:11-17). Jesus forbids John from stopping the man. In essence, telling John, *don't bother him; he is on our side.* Indeed, if his motives or labors were counterfeit, Jesus would have testified to his hypocrisy as he did with the "blind guides" of the time.

Don't marvel at this, for Jesus had many disciples besides "the twelve." Joseph of Arimathea was a disciple of Jesus who provided for his burial (Matthew 27:57-60). Jesus sent 70 disciples out by two to declare the Kingdom of heaven, cast out devils, and heal the sick (Luke 10:1-23). A remnant of disciples stayed after many left him, having their faith challenged after an immense crowd arrived after hearing of Jesus feeding multitudes with fish and bread (John 6:26-68). Let's not forget the owners of the colt and donkey, who regarded Jesus as their Lord, or else they would not have released their animal for the master's use (Luke 19:31). When it comes to walking in freedom, you must choose this day whom you will serve, for there can be no mixture in the life of your holy garments/behavior (Deuteronomy 22:11, Matthew 9:16).

While the devil and his ministers can transform themselves into angels of light, with the

...the enemy has a distinguishable flaw. He can not fake deliverance.

ability to perform lying signs and wonders (2 Corinthians 11:13-15, 2 Thessalonians 2:9-11), the enemy has a distinguishable flaw. He can not fake deliverance! To do so would require satan to cast out satan, which, to him, is no profit to give up ground already acquired for the chance at gaining another. We received a more detailed explanation of this in Matthew's account. Let's read it together.

> *"And Jesus knew their thoughts, and said unto them, Every Kingdom divided against itself is*

brought to desolation; and every city or house di-
vided against itself shall not stand: And if Satan
cast out Satan, he is divided against himself; how
shall then his Kingdom stand? And if I by Beelze-
bub cast out devils, by whom do your children cast
them out? therefore they shall be your judges. But
if I cast out devils by the Spirit of God, then the
Kingdom of God is come unto you. Or else how
can one enter into a strong man's house, and spoil
his goods, except he first bind the strong man? and
then he will spoil his house. He that is not with me
is against me; and he that gathereth not with me
scattereth abroad." (Matthew 12:25-30 KJV)

Jesus describes, in part, the realities of spiritual warfare, teaching that there are only two sides to this conflict. In a two-sided conflict, It becomes apparent whose side you are on when it is clear who your enemy is. Jesus contends with a group of people claiming not to know who he is or his motives. Knowing their hearts, Jesus reasons with them by drawing their attention to who his enemies are—explaining that the devil will not deceive others through his self-defeat. It would be illogical for him to do so. Acts 13:38-39 (ESV) says, *"Let it be known to you therefore, brothers, that through this man forgiveness of sins is proclaimed to you, and by him, everyone who believes is freed from everything from which you could not be freed by the law of Moses."* If satan is being driven out, it is obviously against his will, making it impossible for Jesus to be in alliance with satan, as deliverance is a defining characteristic of The Christ.

Christ came to redeem us from the law's curse and free us from demonic oppression

Today, we have a reason to rejoice because the one who is greater than Moses has come!

and bondage. The law is good because, as a tutor, it taught the people of God what sin was until the teacher arrived to enable us to walk in liberty. Deuteronomy 27:36 says, *"Cursed is he who does not put the words of this law into practice...."* Do you ever wonder why that is? In the first place, the law defined the way of life. Living outside of "the way" was not profitable and, in many cases, naturally illegal for us to indulge in. In cases of judgment, law violators would be stoned to death, and sons of the guilty would suffer shame or be denied temple access for generations. Justice was usually swift and merciless, intending to discourage others from doing the same and stop the influence and agreement of whatever spirit was behind the disobedient act. The law, in this case, is what it looks like to fight spiritual battles with carnal weapons.

The law brings wrath (Romans 4:15), so without the redeeming power of Christ to free those affected, the leaders of God's people could only kill those infected with an evil spirit (Ecclesiastes 8:11), with the hope of saving others who were just as powerless against the enemy's wiles. Today, we have a reason to rejoice because the one who is more significant than Moses has come! Jesus is not the servant; He is the Son described in Hebrews 3:1-6. He is the breaker of Micah 2:13, the yoke destroyer of Isaiah 10:27. For all of the supernatural power exercised by Moses, the patriarchs, and the prophets, no one had displayed such direct dominion over evil spirits. Jesus' willingness and ability to set us free from the enemy is one of the confirming attributes of Christ. *"The people were all so amazed that they asked each other, "What is this? A new teaching—and with authority! He even gives orders to impure spirits, and they obey him" (Mark 1:27 NIV).* Jesus did this because he could spiritually discern the lines that separated friend from foe. Keeping oneself free from the enemy's influence was one of Jesus' most assertive commands (Matthew 5:27-30, 18:6-9).

Trespasses commonly occur when we are left to guess and choose what we want to believe...

One thing my father and forty years of ministry have taught me is that there is a thin line between worship and witchcraft. The borders that separate the two are finely marked in scripture, with the margin of error made easy to trespass when blinded by pride and self-will. Trespasses commonly occur when we are left to guess and choose what we want to believe without the discipline or the direction God provides through his instructions. In doing this, we fall into what Paul described in Romans 1 as those who worship the "created" rather than the creator himself.

> *"You must not make for yourself an idol of any kind or an image of anything in the heavens or on the earth or in the sea." (Exodus 20:4 NLT)*

From the time of Moses until the coming of Christ, we see the warning of Exodus 20:4 being ignored until the sentence is pronounced in Romans 1:21-23; *"For although they knew God, they neither glorified him as God nor gave thanks to him, but their thinking became futile and their foolish hearts were darkened. Although they claimed to be wise, they became fools and exchanged the glory of the immortal God for images made to look like a mortal human being and birds and animals and reptiles."* Humans are made with God-given creative ability. Our gift allows us to turn ideas into reality and tangible plans into masterpieces to be enjoyed by others.

Romans 1 describes how a soul is darkened, not by forgetting God, but by the willing rejection of his holiness. Rejecting God leads to a distorted view of God. Romans 1:21 says that they knew God but did not give glory or thanks to him as God. Instead, verse 23 points out they exchanged the glory (attributes) of the immortal God into images made by things seen in nature. We see this in many ancient and modern religions and beliefs attributing divine qualities or status to animals or elemental forces. On a lighter note, let's take, for instance, the custom of having a team mascot. A mascot implies a team or organization's personified character or values, representing the competitive spirit that the sports club wishes to embody during competition. According to the International University Sports Organization, 'mascot' comes from the French term 'Mascotte,' meaning lucky charm. Scripture goes no further than using images to serve as symbolic illustrations ("Wise as serpents," "harmless as doves," mounted up on "wings as eagles," or "bold as lions").

The slippery slope occurs when an idea grows into an ideal, ultimately becoming an idol. Idols aren't built overnight, but they start when we attribute more reverence to an idea or concept than we should. We are instructed to look to Jesus, the author and finisher of our faith (Hebrews 12:2). Many well-meaning believers incorrectly take that verse to mean keeping a crucifix that immortalizes the image of the dying Christ on the cross. My friends, that image is an inaccurate depiction of who Christ is. Remember, Christ is risen indeed (Luke 24:5-7)! Our "looking upon Christ" is not with natural eyes but through the spiritual lens of revelation that God gives. 2 Corinthians 3:18 Amplified says, *"And we all, with unveiled face, continually seeing as in a mirror the glory of the Lord, are progressively being transformed into His image from [one degree of] glory to [even more] glory, which comes from the Lord, [who is] the Spirit."* On earth, Christ was the full expression of the Godhead bodily(Colossians 2:9). Now, he stands at the right hand of the Father, making intercession for you and me (Romans 8:34, 1 John 2:1). He is our perfect high priest, without end of days holding the new covenant in place by the power of an endless life (Hebrews 7:25).

The slippery slope occurs when an idea grows into an ideal, ultimately becoming an idol.

Images are powerful, especially when they perpetuate a narrative that is not true. We honor the Lord through our faith, not our possessions. At the risk of our friendship, I suggest you remove that crucifix from around your neck and take it off the wall. I'm sure such things are done in reverence but not in truth. Graven images also include paintings. The iconic illustrations of Jesus made famous by the Catholic church have long been proven scripturally inaccurate and incongruent with how Christ would describe himself. As Jesus addressed his doubters who struggled to believe, I encourage you with the same command; *"search the scriptures for they testify of me"* (John 5:39). As was the case with Thomas, the need for tangible evidence does more to erode faith than it does to soothe doubts.

Don't cling to things, cling to God. Jesus had you in mind when he told Thomas, *"Blessed are they who believe and have not (physically) seen"* (John 20:29-31 *emphasis added*). Behind every image is an origin, many of which do not start nor point to God. That's why we must discern what we associate ourselves with, be it the emblems of our possessions, jewelry, or apparel. Some jewelry and apparel are not strictly aesthetic accessories; some represent lifestyle practices and social affiliations, and some serve as cultural relics or spiritual points of contact. Many of our fashions of the day are created by atheist/agnostic artists devoted to alternative lifestyles, which promote sexuality, immorality, and the worship of self.

1 Peter 3:3-4 NLT says, "Don't *be concerned about the outward beauty of fancy hairstyles, expensive jewelry, or beautiful clothes. You should clothe yourselves instead with the beauty that comes from within, the*

> *Don't cling to things, cling to God.*

unfading beauty of a gentle and quiet spirit, which is so precious to God." Remember that "thin line" I told you about? Here it is again. I remember a time in the church where I grew up, women were not allowed to wear any makeup or jewelry. It was widely held that such was not fitting of holiness; some went so far as to misappropriate the name Jezebel to women who seemed to take care of looking attractive. Contrarily, the scriptures highlight the source of true beauty, which never fades, as Proverbs 31:30 teaches. It admonishes believers that beauty comes from a pure heart, not pearls and paint. The work of the Holy Spirit on a person's life is an inside job. By the Holy Spirit, we are to will and do His good pleasure.

However, the use of outward adornments can present a degree of misrepresentation. The

> *The work of the Holy Spirit on a person's life is an inside job.*

Bible talks about carnal distractions as tools used by the seducing spirits, as in Proverbs chapter five, and the pernicious preachers who lure unstable believers away through their lust for things (2 Peter 2:14). To be clear, the Bible did not say that you can not look nice. My father often said, *"Any old barn looks good if you paint it."* There is nothing wrong with touching up our rough patches. Still, our image (reputation) should first be a proper reflection of the God we serve, not the labels we buy; this, too, is vanity.

Exodus 17:14-16 NLT - The Lord Is Your Banner

After the victory, the Lord instructed Moses, "Write this down on a scroll as a permanent reminder, and read it aloud to Joshua: I will erase the memory of Amalek from under heaven." Moses built an altar there and named it Yahweh-Nissi (which means "the Lord is my banner"). He said, "They have raised their fist against the Lord's throne, so now the Lord will be at war with Amalek generation after generation."

As the children of God prevailed against the Amalekites in Exodus 17, we, too, can stand victorious over the enemy by standing under God's banner of protection. 1 Peter 5:6 teaches that we must "Humble ourselves under the mighty hand of God, that he may exalt us in due time ."Joshua humbled himself and depended on Moses' outstretched hands of intercession. At God's request, Gideon went to battle with less than 1% of his army, entrusting the fight to God. David refused to wear King Saul's armor into battle but entrusted his life to the commander of the heavenly host to guide his sling and stones. What was true for them is true for us today;

this battle belongs to the Lord. We are thankful for friendly help, mental intelligence, and reasonable strength, but we stand by God's grace. God will share his glory with nothing or no one.

> *"You adulterers! Don't you realize that friendship with the world makes you an enemy of God? I say it again: If you want to be a friend of the world, you make yourself an enemy of God. Do you think the Scriptures have no meaning? They say that God is passionate that the spirit he has placed within us should be faithful to him." (James 4:4-5 NLT)*

In everything, we must first seek God's Kingdom and his way of doing things. As God's representatives on the earth, we must be careful of what represents us. I remember when my dad had just bought a beautiful new home. It was the biggest one he'd ever had up to that point. My father had many friends, and some gave housewarming gifts to help furnish and decorate the home. My father was very gracious and gladly received blessings from friends and family. One day, a realtor friend of my father came by the house to discuss other business matters. As we walked by the foyer, she stopped. Bishop, she said. "Do you know what that is?!" She pointed to a figure in the sitting room; we thought it was an accent piece of art. She told us of this figure's cultural history and spiritual significance in the part of the world it originates from, where she was also born. I thank God she loved us enough to challenge what she knew did not represent who we were. Immediately, my father threw it out.

Most people do not inten-
tionally adopt things or prac-

In everything, we must first seek God's Kingdom, and his way of doing things.

tices that grant the enemy access to our lives. My intent here is not to discourage you but to encourage vigilance. If it can happen to a Bishop who wanted to honor a well-meaning gift, it can happen to any of us caught unawares. As saints of God, we stand in the newness of his life and under God's protection. We must remain vigilant, for even God's protection does not discourage satan's pursuit. By nature, satan is highly possessive and legalistic regarding the territory he once occupied in your life.

In many cases, he still regards you as an old house he's determined to return (Mark 12:44). We see a scriptural parallel to this in Genesis 31:17-42. Jacob, determined to live free, broke away from the exploitation he suffered under the hand of his uncle Laban. He quickly gathered his household and returned to his father's country. During the move, unbeknownst to Jacob, his wife Rachel had secretly taken with her the household gods of her father.

When Laban realized Jacob had left in the middle of the night, he was determined to track him down to prevent his leaving. While resting in the heat of his pursuit, God spoke to Laban directly, warning him not to touch Jacob and do him no harm. Even though Jocab was blessed and protected by God, Laban continued his pursuit. When Laban finally caught up with Jacob, as mad as he was, he knew that he could do nothing to harm him unprovoked. Laban, being the trickster he was, couldn't justify his heated pursuit of Jacob, except by claiming his rights of ownership of the idols his daughter Rachel had stowed away in her belongings.

...even with God's blessing, we should not give the enemy any cause to claim any part of our lives.

The story's moral is that even with God's blessing, we should not give the enemy any cause to claim any part of our lives. Just as it benefited Laban to keep Jacob as a servant, it is to the enemy's advantage that we stay weak and ignorant of his devices. That is why we must be zealous to repent whenever God gives us more grace for understanding, inviting us to walk closer with him in holiness. Be careful about what you allow in your house, on your clothes, and especially on your body. The desire to be seen as culturally relevant has cost many Kingdom people dearly. Objects can serve as physical points of contact of faith despite what a person believes. Objects can attract familiar spirits as a mark of an unholy alliance or carry the blessing of righteous prayer. Let it not be said that we wore mixed garments of compromise but took to heart the charge to show God's praises in everything we do. Be not conformed to this world but be transformed by renewing your mind so that you may prove (with your actions) the good, perfect, and acceptable will of God. If God is your banner, don't let your liberty become a stumbling block to you or those around you. Take not unto yourself any cursed thing unless you and all that pertains to you become accursed.

Chapter 9

The Art of Warfare

For we wrestle not against flesh and blood, but against principalities, against powers, against the rulers of the darkness of this world, against spiritual wickedness in high places.

(Ephesians 6:12 KJV)

***

Paul's language in Ephesians 6:12, such as "principalities" and "rulership," suggests geographical territories that demarcate various levels of influence or control a person or group may share. Demonic spirits are assigned explicitly to countries, cities, towns, and communities by their kingdom structure and order to disrupt God's angelic host and our earthly purpose. Looking at our world through this view, we can understand how such spiritual alignments affect us.

Though murder, vice, poverty, and death exist everywhere, why do some nations have a reputation for certain evils more than others? Some nations are known as conquerors, while others are synonymous with poverty. Some nations are highly secular, while others boast of their spiritual culture and religious tolerance or lack thereof.

An environmental survey of any area, large or small, will reflect the leadership of that region, be it a country, community, church, or club. Leadership is the pervading spiritual influence or intent expressed upon or through a people, place, or agenda. Notice I'm defining leadership and not "leader." Leadership is spiritual, as listed in Romans 12:8. A leader is a single man or woman presently charged with the task of administering an office or charge of leadership. Eventually, that person will die or retire, and if not for the help of God, things will go as they did after that person is gone, just as they had before. A human leader is not without authority. However, we hold the terrestrial keys that allow and disallow any leadership / spiritual agenda philosophy to perpetuate and grow (Matthew 18:18).

Demonic spirits are assigned...by their kingdom structure and order to disrupt God's angelic host and our earthly purpose.

As Christians, we are charged to Influence the area we inhabit with God's Leadership agenda, "The Kingdom" (Mark 24:14). However, we can be deceived into serving as gates of hell for the enemy's use, propagating his thoughts and agenda into the spaces we occupy (Matthew 16:23). Environmental influence of spiritual forces is exceedingly broad, essentially encapsulating everything we have discussed so far. For something to be categorized as "the spirit of a place or environment" that place must be permeated with that theme or attitude. My goal is to make you aware of the principles of this reality, how it impacts you as an individual, and how you can best navigate to avoid unnecessary snares.

The Principle of Principalities

Daniel was a member of the generation of Israel that was led into captivity to Babylon as prophesied by the prophet Jeremiah. During those seventy years, Daniel interpreted the dream of King Neubukanezar that showed the cascading world powers that would follow him (Daniel 2:36-43). By chapter ten, many years later, Nebuchadnezzar has passed, and Babylon is under the rule of the Medo-Persian empire, a conquest led by King Cyrus II. Daniel is in anguish over the state of his people, and he seeks God for direction. God favored Daniel and was granted visitation from the angel

Gabriel with God's reply. Let's look closely at what the delivery of that message revealed about the supernatural implications of Daniel's geography.

> *"Then he said to me, "Do not fear, Daniel, for from the first day that you set your heart to understand, and to humble yourself before your God, your words were heard; and I have come because of your words. But the prince of the Kingdom of Persia withstood me twenty-one days; and behold, Michael, one of the chief princes, came to help me, for I had been left alone there with the kings of Persia." (Daniel 10:12-13 NKJV)*

Gabriel is a member of God's heavenly host. An angel of God, Psalm 103:20 describes as one who excels in strength and does the commandments of God. In the preceding verses of Daniel 10, we read how Daniel fell as a dead man at the mere entrance of Gabriel's presence. I emphasize this point to draw the immense contrast between a human and an angel of God. Gabriel admitted that his delay was due to a 21-day stalemate with the prince of the Kingdom of Persia. I assure you, he was not talking about King Cyrus but the spirit behind the Medo-Persian empire. We know this spirit was an enemy of the Lord because it openly opposed Daniel and his God-given task. This dark spirit was so great and powerful that it manifested the leadership agenda of an entire earthly kingdom!

We see a similar example of spiritual wickedness and its impact on a local and personal scale found in Mark Chapter 5. Jesus and his disciples travel to the country of the Gadarenes. Jesus was encountered on the shore by a demonically oppressed man living in the graveyard, suffering fits of rage and cutting himself. In this startling discourse, the spirit oppressing the man identified itself as Legion, referring to the amount of collaborating spirits at work tormenting the man. Jesus, fixing his gaze on the man, was determined to see him free. Knowing that their time was near an end, Legion began to bargain. Let's read together what Legion's actual point of concern was.

> "When he saw Jesus from afar, he ran and worshiped Him. And he cried out with a loud voice and said, "What have I to do with You, Jesus, Son of the Most High God? I implore You by God that You do not torment me." For He said to him, "Come out of the man, unclean spirit!" Then He asked him, "What is your name?" And he an-

swered, saying, "My name is Legion; for we are many." <u>Also he begged Him earnestly that He would not send them out of the country.</u>" (Mark 5:6-10 NKJV emphasis added)

Legion was no prince of Persia, but he was determined to stay in the country region of the Gaderens. Met with greater power and authority, Legion resigned to letting go of that man, just as long as he could keep his geographical hold on that area. Being the Son of Man, Jesus allowed Legion to go into the pigs. This is important to note because it is within our rights and authority to declare what is permitted and what is not in our homes, places of work, and worship. Psalm 115:16 NIV says, "The highest heavens belong to the Lord, but the earth he has given to mankind." Whatever spirit impacts our earthly territory does so because we either permitted it or have been passive in our negligence.

> *Whatever spirit impacts our earthly territory does so because we either gave it permission or have been passive in our negligence.*

Have you ever wondered why Jesus allowed Legion to enter the pigs but remain in the area? Remember, the man fell and worshiped Jesus. Still, the Gaderens ultimately demanded that Jesus leave from their coast (Mark 5:17). I believe wherever there is true worship, God will honor the promise of 2 Chronicles 7:14. Still, the people must first corporately humble themselves, seek God, and repent before the land can be healed. Since only the oppressed man was willing to do this, he was freed while his country remained in darkness.

Before we storm off to tear down every perceived demonic stronghold, we must understand that there are levels to spiritual warfare. First, we must save ourselves from "this untoward generation," securing personal freedom is the first step to large-scale victory. It's dangerous for any man to think more of himself than he should (Galatians 6:3). The devil is not fooled by religious theatrics; shout, cry, bind, and lose as you may, you are only fooling yourself when you operate outside your jurisdiction. The enemy sets his counterfeit Kingdom up against God and his people, but we are not without defense. There are angels of God everywhere; just as there is a temporal political and military hierarchy in the world, God's army battles with us and for us in the unseen heavenly realm aligned to war against the ranks of the Kingdom of darkness (Ephesians 6:12).

Turn again to Daniel 10:20 KJV for a vivid picture of this

securing personal freedom is the first step to large-scale victory reality: *"Then said he, Knowest thou wherefore I come unto thee? and now will I return to fight with the prince of Persia: and when I am gone forth, lo, the prince of Grecia shall come."* Historically, the Grecian (Greek) Empire eventually succeeded the Medo-Persian Empire as the next world power, much to the credit of Alexander the Great as the earthly face of that heavenly change of power. However, as scripture shows, leaders come and go, but the "principal spirit" behind their leadership never dies. These demonic spirits manipulate and control what goes on within their respective jurisdictions. They are at work in the nations of today and will play their part on the last day as the seven-headed beast of Rev 13 with its ten horns (leaders) and crowns. These majorly influential spirits are how some areas come to be classified or known as high-level immoral zones of activity. If proper care is not taken, innocent people living in such regions may become victims of their environment or complicit in conforming to the pervading culture.

Be Not Conformed To This World

"I pray not that thou shouldest take them out of the world, but that thou shouldest keep them from the evil. They are not of the world, even as I am not

of the world. Sanctify them through thy truth: thy
word is truth." John 17:15-17 KJV

We have been given the power to change our atmosphere by the words we speak and the company we keep. This is important for believers, not as a religious cliche but as a necessity for living victoriously. The impact of our external environment begins with the personal indwelling of the Holy Spirit. In so doing, God expands his abode, making our very bodies his temple (1 Corinthians 6:19). This is what Jesus spoke of when speaking to the woman at the well as she contested the location of acceptable worship. In John 4:21 & 23 (KJV), *"Jesus saith unto her, woman, believe me, the hour cometh, when ye shall neither in this mountain, nor yet at Jerusalem, worship the Father. But the hour cometh, and now is, when the true worshippers shall worship the Father in spirit and in truth: for the Father seeketh such to worship him."* What's so awesome about what Jesus says here is that it speaks to the global spread of true worship and the international unity of worshipers in truth.

The impact of our external environment begins with the personal indwelling of the Holy Spirit.

When earthly agreement exists, victory (especially spiritual warfare) can be realized. Jesus reiterates his point in Matthew

18:19-20; *"Again I say unto you, That if two of you shall agree on earth as touching anything that they shall ask, it shall be done for them of my Father which is in heaven. For where two or three are gathered together in my name, there am I in the midst of them."* I can't express how much I pray for the spirit of love and unity to abound in my ministry. The enemy keeps us defeated by keeping us divided. When we align our hearts to what God wants, we automatically find ourselves in accord with one another. Just as on the day of Pentecost in Acts 2:1, there is a spiritual significance and power in being on "one accord and in one place." I was always taught that there is strength in numbers. Proverb 14:28 says, "In the multitude of people is the king's honor: but in the want of people is the destruction of the prince."

> *there is a spiritual significance and power in being on "one accord and in one place."*

I ponder when we loose-ly declare scriptural references like "one can chase a thousand, two can put ten thousand to flight (Deuteronomy 32:30)," yet decline corporate prayer meetings and worship services. To make it out of our messes, we must seek out the environments we should be in. Church for believers is a must. Members of my church know that I am quick to reference Hebrews 10:25; *"Not forsaking the assembling of ourselves together, as the manner of some is; but exhorting one another: and so much the more, as ye see the day approaching"* (KJV). Some may never see the value in the community that church provides, but we draw strength from one another. We are responsible for encouraging one another in the faith as we see the day of the Lord's return soon come. Some will argue that they don't need encouragement; they pray and read their Bible at home.

> *Sometimes, the best way to change your situation is to change your seat.*

There may be some exceptions among the sick and the shut-in, but 1 John 1:6-7 says, "If we say that we have fellowship with Him, and walk in darkness, we lie and do not practice the truth. But if we walk in the light as He is in the light, we have fellowship with one another, and the blood of Jesus Christ His Son cleanses us from all sin." Sometimes, the best way to change your situation is to change your seat.

Death At A Funeral

"When Jesus arrived at the official's home, he saw the noisy crowd and heard the funeral music. "Get out!" he told them. "The girl isn't dead; she's only asleep." But the crowd laughed at him. After the crowd was put outside, however, Jesus went in and took the girl by the hand, and she stood up! The re-

*port of this miracle swept through the entire coun-
tryside." (Matthew 9:23-26 NLT)*

Years ago, during my father's pastorate, a family in the
church suffered the loss of their young adult child due to a
shooting incident. It was sudden, tragic, and an incredible
blow to the family and those of us who grew up with him.
The family had the funeral, and the congregation supported them wherever possible, as is our custom. Days after the
funeral, many people occasionally stopped by and showed
concern, while others also brought food. Years of ministry
have revealed just how delicate a person is while moving
through the stages of mourning. During such a time, having
the right people around you is crucial, saying the right things
and speaking words of comfort, encouragement, and wisdom
into your life.

As time continued, the bereavement visits didn't stop; they
turned into something else. Visitors continued to come by
but began doing more than "saying hi." Remember, I said
how vulnerable grief and mourning can leave us. As wolves
seek out the weak and the wounded, the enemy is the same
when he walks about. He has no problem exploiting our pain
to find opportunities to infiltrate our lives. The family was
emotionally weak and spiritually spent. Anyone in their posi-

tion would be more depressed than discerning; they expected friends to visit, not enemies.

Merciless in his pursuit of our joy, satan will use a friend as

> As wolves seek out the weak and the wounded, the enemy is the same when he walks about.

freely as he would a foe to poison your heart. It all depends on who can get closest to your ear. The visitations continued and began to grow in regularity and frequency. People started taking greater liberty in how often they visited and how long they stayed. Greetings such as "I made you dinner" became code for "I'm on the way." How are you doing?" became the password for gossip. What began as caring conversations degraded into carnal chit-chat. Fellowship became factions as people started "hanging out" instead of checking in.

One day, my father arose, disturbed with great concern for the family. Immediately, he called one of the elders to meet him at his office. As he entered, my father pointed sternly in his direction, and with force, he said, *"Go over there and get those people out of that house!"* My father turned to me and began sharing his vision. In his dream, he saw the house entirely packed with visitors. In addition to the people, he could see various spirits coming, going, and staying as visitors sat talking. It was as if a shadow was forming over that home that wasn't there before. Upon arriving at the house, we could see groups of people, most of whom were not talking with the family but among themselves. They were even noticeably paired off in respective groups. I began to see members of these groups shared lifestyles and proclivities they once fought to keep hidden. It became naturally evident what the Lord warned my father about spiritually. The enemy was looking to take advantage of this moment of weakness to establish and legitimize connections and relationships that would have been hard to accomplish at church. It was no longer about the family but the point of reference their house now provided on the occasion of the funeral for the enemy to have his way. If we had not intervened, that home would have been turned into that family's prison of depression and bondage.

The Blessing of Home Field Advantage

But when Elisha, the man of God, heard that the king of Israel had torn his clothes in dismay, he sent this message to him: "Why are you so upset? Send Naaman to me, and he will learn that there is a true prophet here in Israel." (2 Kings 5:8 NLT)

Jesus' guidance was meant to ensure their safety and their success.

It is commonplace in ministry to make house calls to the sick, shut in, and visit the orphan and imprisoned. Whenever a saint of God ventures into such work, they must be mindful of the environments they traverse. When Jesus sent out his disciples to missions, be it the twelve in Matthew 10:1-15 or the seventy-two in Luke 10:1-23, he guided them in fulfilling their mandate. Jesus' guidance was meant to ensure their safety and their success.

1. **Don't Go Alone:** Firstly, they were to travel two by two (Luke 10:1). The two by two partner ministry pattern is seen throughout the Apostles' later ministry. Whether it was Paul and Silas, Peter and John, or Paul and Barnabas, the two-by-two principle wasn't a beginner's training wheel but the practical wisdom of a trained workman (Ecclesiastes 4:9-10).

2. **Stay In Your Lane**: Secondly, it is a matter of life and death that we obey the given scope of our ministry and purpose (Luke 10:1,3-4 | Matthew 10:5-6). In both accounts, the latitude Jesus gave them was intended for a specific geographical area and a group of people. In Luke's account, the Seventy-two were being sent to the towns Jesus planned

to visit personally. In Matthew, the target audience was the lost sheep of Israel, who would have a historical point of reference to the simple message they were sent to proclaim. As we depend on Jesus to lead us today, it is essential to go only where God tells us to go, work only where he is working, and do what he tells us to do. We must work in partnership with God, focused on the task at hand with a singular focus.

This should challenge us to avoid becoming preoccupied with publicity or juggling competing priorities dur-

...it is essential to go only where God tells us to go, work only where he is working...

ing such work. Jesus even told them not to shake hands with anyone they may meet on the road. The disciple's instructions are not a license for us to take ourselves too seriously while being impolite to those not of priority. Instead, it teaches the level of focus and intentionality we should have in doing the work of God. Let us lay aside every weight that hinders us. Our good intentions are just as good as any other desire satan can use to exploit us. The enemy is equally skilled in tempting us to sin through virtues, as with vices. Obedience to God is fulfilled not only by what we do but how we go about doing it.

3. **Go Where There is Agreement:** Jesus instructs them to go only where there is agreement (Luke 10:5-8, 10-11 | Matthew 10:11-14). We must discern the spirit of the environments we walk into. The prevailing spirit of a place will determine if those there will be receptive or repelled by the gospel and the will of God. When entering a town, Jesus instructs his disciples in Matthew to search out a "worthy person" and stay at his house the entire time they are doing ministry there. In Luke, when entering a home, Jesus tells them to find someone who promotes peace so that their peace can rest on them. God is a God of order, recognizing authority in heaven and on earth. The house of the worthy man legitimizes Godly influence in that town, just as the agreeable person of peace permits the work of God in that home. Even though the disciples would still face the enemy's opposition, they were positioned to prevail. Traveling two by two, they needed another soul to agree with them, changing the environment with a three-fold cord, which is not easily broken (Ecclesiastes 4:12).

4. **Declare, Don't Debate:** Finally, the disciples would be free to declare the Kingdom, not debate it (Luke 10:8-11 | Matthew 10:7-8). Jesus said, freely you have received, so freely give. Preach the word, heal the sick, cast out evil spirits, and declare the Kingdom of God. This is made possible when

the environment is aligned with God's will. When two or three are gathered in Jesus' name, he promised to be in the midst of us. When we dwell together in unity, as described in Psalms 133, a cascade of anointing is poured out because of the agreement that enables God to "Command" a blessing to rest in a specific place. On the day I stood up as the Pastor, I declared Scripture Cathedral a "Praise First Church"! Praise changes the atmosphere; we enter his gates with thanksgiving and draw closer in his courts with our praise. Once we are in the King's court, we are blessed with the privilege to ask of him for everything we need.

Every first Sunday of the month, we make it a point to dedicate that time and space for healing and deliverance. Of course, we believe God can heal, set free, and deliver anytime he wants. First Sundays are the time we set aside to celebrate the healer that he is. Apostle C. L. Long, our founder, walked in a heavy healing and deliverance ministry for over 40 years. Since becoming a pastor, I've experienced a similar mantle resting on my life, growing in degrees. As with my father, I'm beginning to see the same growth in me. I've prayed and witnessed God heal people, surgeries canceled, husbands and wives reconciled, and children restored to the care and authority of their parents. In every case, I prayed intensely to be led by the Lord in what I say and do.

One day, my office received a call requesting that I come and pray for an individual suffering from what I was convinced to be intense demonic oppression. This person was not a church member, but I was somewhat familiar with who they were. I counseled the individual over the phone and gathered as much information as possible. I resolved to pray for this person, but I submitted to God whether or not I would make a house call and see them. I knew that if I went, I would not be going alone. I took my time in prayer regarding this particular request. I wanted to ensure I was aligned with the course The Lord had plotted for me. Still, I had no peace to go. I did not feel released by God to make this house call. I had the ministry support willing to assist me, yet while praying to God for permission, he gave me the wisdom to discern whether or not this was a house of agreement.

For prayer of any kind to be successful, it must be done in faith, according to God's word. During my counseling with the individual, it was not evident that the individual held personal faith in the name of Jesus. Instead, I felt this was a last resort dependent solely on my belief in God. Whatever the reason, my peace never seemed to release me to make this house call. I needed to ensure I was working with God and not trusting my inclinations. Next, I looked for agreement.

There must be faith on both sides for deliverance to come. I reached out to the individual to give them my answer. I told the person that I would pray for them, but they must come to see me. "Come to the church, and I'll pray for you," I said. Upon hearing this, they groaned in acknowledgment about how much they knew they should and were making plans to come to church more often. I remained quiet and let them continue. After all their explanations, they never confirmed when they would show up. Until now, the invitation still stands, but I have received no visits since offering my invitation. Suddenly, the plea for prayer no longer seemed so urgent.

Some may charge me with not being accommodating or not being willing to meet the person where they were. Every scenario is different and requires spiritual discernment and tact. My request for the person to meet me at the church was strategic for all involved. First, it moved the battle to my home turf. I have the support and prayers of my staff and the saints to cover us both in prayer. My church is a sacred space; I have God's covering over my church. We'll discuss the importance of sacred space a little later. As for my sanctuary, I've anointed every threshold and every pew, praying that God blesses everyone who enters. I prayed that every heart entered with praise, doubters be empowered to believe, and that no one with a need leave the same while those seeking the Holy Ghost would be filled. The candidate's obedience to come would have been a personal act of faith on their part to bring them out of their house and into agreement with me. Unfortunately, the person never showed up.

In 2 Kings 5, Naaman was foreign to the God of Israel, but it was the prophet's command to come to Israel to receive his healing. God intended that Naaman did not doubt how he came about his healing. Syrian captain or not, his soul was converted with the testimony that the God of Israel had healed him. Israel became his sacred space, and he requested to take as much of Israel's soil with him as he returned home (2 Kings 5:17-18). The woman with the issue of blood in Mark 5:25 saw fit to leave her home to press through her pain and a crowd of people to receive her healing. Even the man oppressed by Legion thought enough to go from the tombs and meet Jesus on the shore. The fact is, I knew the person was capable of making the trip, but their unwillingness to come revealed their inability to believe. In hindsight, going to their house would have been a bad idea in light of the spirit's direction. Indeed, there is strength in numbers.

Sacred Space

But will God indeed dwell on the earth? behold, the heaven and heaven of heavens cannot contain thee; how much less this house that I have builded? Yet have thou respect unto the prayer of thy servant, and to his supplication, O Lord my God, to hearken unto the cry and to the prayer, which thy servant prayeth before thee to day: That thine eyes may be open toward this house night and day, even toward the place of which thou hast said, My name shall be there: that thou mayest hearken unto the prayer which thy servant shall make toward this place. 1 Kings 8:27-29 KJV

As service concluded one night, my staff escorted the guest minister to his guest room. Exhilarated by the service, he exclaims, "I can't explain it; I've never preached like that before!" That phrase has become a recurring trend among many guest pastors and speakers visiting our church to preach. They would use church vocabulary to say, "Your pulpit is hot." A term used to describe a place where the burden of preaching isn't a burden at all. My pulpit has an anointing that provides an unction for preaching that makes the supernatural work of its purpose possible to sincere servants. Every minister delivering the word of God should pray for such grace, with God as your help in this regard. We can truly stand as his vessel and be both a witness and partaker of God's great power. My father understood this and took preaching and teaching God's word seriously. Growing up, I often marveled how my father could minister a minimum of 5 times a week (3 times on Sunday), sometimes while sick, and still deliver some of his most prolific sermons. He was indeed a man of great study but of more profound prayer. Through prayer and consecration, God answered his prayer to extend grace to him whenever he stepped into his pulpit to preach.

Over the years and through his work in making disciples, that grace was extended to those who stood in that sacred space upon invitation. Often, my father would tell others selflessly, "I like good preaching; that's why I asked you to preach." He knew where his help came from and was not intimidated by another's presentation style or ability to "move a crowd." He confidently told me, "I know I'm not the most 'gifted preacher,' but one thing is for sure - I'm anointed." In part, that anointing resulted from his consecrated effort to sanctify his pulpit and set it aside for preaching only; in turn, God blessed that place with a "preaching anointing." I've witnessed world-renowned ministers to trembling youths giving their trial sermons, all having their gifts blessed because of the altar they were standing on (Matthew 23:19).

In 1 Kings 8, the temple of the Lord is built, and the decrees are spoken over it during its dedication ceremony. The man of God prays, acknowledging God's presence fills the heavens and the entire earth. He concedes that nothing made with man's hand can contain God. However, he says, "Yet have thou respect unto the prayer of thy servant...." My father taught me a lesson I will never forget, "It is through consecrated efforts that we have access to God." As with Jacob and many others, we build altars and pulpits as consecrated places to hear and meet with God (Genesis 28:16).

The consecrated act of prayer gives us access to the heavenly Kingdom's power and plans for earthly affairs (Mathew 6:10). Fasting is a consecrated effort by making ourselves available to the Lord for particular use and effectiveness (Matthew 6:16-18). Even coming together and attending church services is a consecrated act, although many have diluted it into a form and activity of little meaning. Nothing can be further from the truth. 1 Kings 8:27-29 shows us in principle how God will honor places of worship dedicated to his glorious purpose.

In John 4:19-24 Jesus expounds on sacred space while talking to the woman at the well. He explains that God is still looking to grace his temple with his presence! Now, because of the redemptive work of Christ, we are the temple of the living God. More splendid than Solomon's temple ever was, we are the living stones by which Christ himself is building a spiritual house of a holy priesthood, spread across the entire world (1 Peter 2:5). Those who have a partial understanding of this truth argue against their need for the church and are resigned to pray at home. Such deconstructionist views rob the believer of much more than fellowship, but the gifts and promises Christ provides corporately to enrich each individual. Though God is not bound by space, he favors places sanctified through consecrated efforts. Hebrews 10:25 encourages us not to forsake our gathering together. We draw strength from one another when we encourage each other daily. We are all members of one body, made interdependent on one another. The commanded blessing of Psalm 133:1-3 had also occurred at Pentecost. The spirit came as they obeyed the corporate command to remain in one place (Acts 2:1-4).

Jesus told them in Luke 24:49 (NKJV), "Behold, I send the Promise of My Father upon you; but tarry in the city of Jerusalem until you are endued with power from on high" (emphasis added). Everything God does can't be streamed, but it must be experienced. Those who understand the power of corporate worship endure persecution from those who don't. Those who received the Holy Spirit at Pentecost were soon chided by outside onlookers (other Jewish worshipers) and marked as a group of people who may have had too much wine to drink. In today's time, it is known as the *"it doesn't take all of that"* critique, asserting that God can do anything, anywhere, with anyone at any time, which is true. God only moves where we are aligned with his purpose (Romans 8:28); however, if we stay home instead of joining the group for prayer or livestream instead of serving personally, we surrender our place of favor for a place of pleasure.

> *Your blessing is in the house!*
> *Your healing is in the body!*
> *Your purpose is to play your part, not cut yourself off.*

Notwithstanding the legitimate reasons, I've heard every excuse from preachers to lay members trying to justify their lack of corporate unity. In the end, as my father would say, "All excuses are lies." Paul was "present in spirit" through his hand-delivered letters as he was hindered by prison or peril. Such is not the case for many of us today; instead, we are most likely hindered by our lack of priority. I must clarify the importance of surrounding ourselves with the right people and places for our daily deliverance and victory. In Matthew 18:20, Jesus promised his presence to those who united in his name. We cannot receive some blessings at home alone when God calls us to come together to receive them. The enemy fights to keep us from this promise by playing on our fears, pride, and self-importance. I've counseled individuals through divorces, financial loss, family tragedy, personal offenses, health challenges, and career setbacks. In every case, the enemy relentlessly finds an advantage over a weak soul.

One of the wiles of the enemy's design is entertaining the idea that it would be more manageable to leave the church and seclude ourselves from healthy relationships that hold us accountable. There is a two-fold mystery to pain. On the one hand, while it is unmistakably genuine, it has its way of revealing the falsehoods in and around us. We learn the truth about our strengths and weaknesses in our darkest hour. There are some blows life dishes out that will cause you to despair of life, but we must not give up on God! Your blessing is in the house! Your healing is in the body! Your purpose is to play your part, not cut yourself off. Just as there are environments to avoid, there are environments to seek out. 1 John 1:7 (NKJV) says, "But if we walk in the light as He is in the light, we have fellowship with one another, and the blood of Jesus Christ His Son cleanses us from all sin."

A final warning concerning death, mourning, and funeral ceremonies: Transference of spirits can also occur through certain burial functions. Demons don't die when people die; when any person they possess dies, these demons would certainly leave such bodies to look for another person or persons to inhabit. They always need a human container to house them. People who work in the mortuary or hospital are advised to learn how to conduct self-deliverance exercises.

Better sanctified, than sorry. During a burial ceremony, some people come around as if they mean to sympathize with the bereaved. Still, they come armed with the wrong motives—familiar spirits attack by seeking to grow connections rooted in trauma and pain, not God's truth. The enemy is ruthless and cares nothing for those grieving loved ones. Christians shouldn't be ignorant of satan's devices but be fully alert. Remember that Satan has a unique way of striking during a bereavement period. We all suffer a degree of vulnerability when found in a low state mentally or emotionally. A demonic attack in such times is dangerous for a person with a minimal prayer life.

Immediately after a grand burial ceremony, whether you're a minister or a newly born-again Christian, please try to conduct comprehensive deliverance on you and your family. *Better sanctified than sorry.*

Prayer of Deliverance

Please say this prayer with me over yourself for your deliverance:

> *Father, I come to you in the name of Jesus Christ.*
> *I submit to your word and your authority over my life.*
> *I thank you that the blood of Jesus cleanses me of my sins.*
> *I repent of every choice, action, and agreement with everything contrary to your will. [name the sin you are aware of]*
> *Father, I break all generational curses of pride, rebellion, lust, poverty, witchcraft, idolatry, death, destruction, failure, sickness, and infirmity in the name of Jesus.*
> *I command all spirits of hurt, rejection, fear, anger, wrath, sadness, depression, discouragement, grief, bitterness, and unforgiveness to come out in the name of Jesus.*
> *I command all spirits of guilt, shame, and condemnation to come out in the name of Jesus.*

I command all spirits of addiction to come out in the name of Jesus.

I command all spirits from my past that hinder my present and future to go and never return in the name of Jesus.

I command all ancestral spirits that entered through my ancestors to come out in the name of Jesus.

I command all hidden spirits hiding in any part of my life to come out in the name of Jesus.

With this prayer, Jesus, I praise your name and count it all done.

AMEN

Chapter 10

Demonic Strongholds

Groupings

(For the weapons of our warfare are not carnal, but mighty through God to the pulling down of strong holds;) Casting down imaginations, and every high thing that exalteth itself against the knowledge of God, and bringing into captivity every thought to the obedience of Christ.
(2 Corinthians 10:4-5 KJV)

***

We must never forget that we are in a war, and the primary battlefield of this war is fought in the mind (soul). Militarily, a stronghold is a place fortified to protect one against attack. Spiritually speaking, it's a place where a particular cause or belief is vigorously defended or upheld. The enemy aims to infiltrate the territory of our soul and mind to erect these mental structures that first make us incapable of discerning between right and wrong.

Strongholds and their root thoughts and feelings often produce inroads to demonic oppression through a sustained skewed view of the world and God's word. If the enemy falls short of preventing a person from believing in God, the second best thing is to limit their growth and effectiveness in God.

Stifling a believer is done by clouding a person's belief in God's promises and character.

If the enemy falls short of preventing a person from believing in God, the second best thing is to limit their growth and effectiveness in God.

Strongholds create unnecessary strain and frustration for an individual and those around them.

As 2 Corinthians 10:4-5 explains, strongholds are the ideas, arguments, and perspectives that do not come from God but are lies promoted by the enemy. As we've discussed, whenever the enemy speaks, he is lying. However, strongholds are powerful because they are lies we have come to believe and agree with. That is why they are described as the high things (mental constructs) that raise themselves to an adversarial position against what's known of God. A stronghold's goal is to keep you from coming into the knowledge of God. As we discuss further, we will survey only a partial list to illuminate their influence's broad potential impact. Much of what you find listed may sound similar, yet they differ slightly in how they manifest. It is essential to be careful and sensitive in discerning which stronghold you may face.

REBELLION

1 Samuel 15:23 For rebellion is as the sin of witchcraft, and stubbornness is as iniquity and idolatry. Because thou hast rejected the word of the Lord, he hath also rejected thee from being king.

- Self-will

- Stubbornness

- Strife

- Factions

- Divisions

- Anger/Arguments

- Independent spirit

- Unteachable

PRIDE

Jeremiah 9:23 This is what the LORD says: "Let not the wise boast of their wisdom or the strong boast of their strength or the rich boast of their riches,

- Vanity

- Self-righteousness

- Self-centered

- Insensitivity

- Materialism

- Unteachable

- Seeks positions

- Selfish ambition

SEXUAL IMPURITY

1 Corinthians 6:18 Flee from sexual immorality. Every other sin a person commits is outside the body, but the sexually immoral person sins against his own body.

- Lust

- Seductiveness

- Masturbation

- Fornication

- Adultery

- Sexual Disorders

- Homosexuality

- Pornography

Remember, you shall know the truth, and the truth shall make you free. Knowing this, the enemy wants to keep you bound by lies. He wants to keep you in the dark about God's intentions for your life, trapping you in a lower quality of living where he has the advantage over you. In Matthew 6:22-23 NLT, Jesus says, *"Your eye is like a lamp that provides light for your body. When your eye is healthy, your whole body is filled with light. But when your eye is unhealthy, your whole body is filled with darkness. And if the light you think you have is actually darkness, how deep that darkness is!"*

One of the factors that make breaking down strongholds so tricky is that much prayer and faith labor must be done to unlearn a lie for truth to be planted and given time to grow. I've seen people with extraordinary callings on their lives become stifled by the enemy due to them picking up belief systems and frames of mind that prevented them from living up to their God-given potential. I've seen believers, full of zeal, exaggerate their place within the mystical body of Christ, devalue church attendance, and neglect the gathering of the saints as Hebrews 10:25 instructs. Their faith soon deteriorates into frustration as they regard leadership and accountability as too restrictive and demanding. I've seen those enamored by prophetic giftings, seemingly devoted chiefly to the voice of the Lord. However, their lack of love and submission harbors a religious spirit that makes it hard for them to hear any other voice but their own.

I've seen leaders never realize their potential in ministry because of their battle with fear and poverty. Though they have everything needed to trust God, they volunteer for over-time and take on additional jobs in the name of prosperity. In reality, the spirit of mammon has tricked them into finding more security in a paycheck than in doing the work of God. The thing about strongholds is that they "raise themselves up" against whatever God says is right. Whenever I challenge a stronghold, I get an excuse as to why they can not obey what they know is right. Whatever the reason is, "I'm working late," "That's just the way I am," or "God knows my heart," they're all excuses, and all excuses are lies. Lies are the ties the enemy uses to keep us bound.

REJECTION

2 Samuel 9:7-8 And David said unto him,
Fear not: for I will surely shew thee kindness for
Jonathan thy father's sake, and will restore thee
all the land of Saul thy father; and thou shalt
eat bread at my table continually. And he bowed

himself, and said, What is thy servant, that thou
shouldest look upon such a dead dog as I am?

- Addictions

- Seeking acceptance

- Compulsions

- Unworthiness

- Withdrawal

- Self Hate

DECEIT

Colossians 2:8 Beware lest any man spoil you
through philosophy and vain deceit, after the tradition of men, after the rudiments of the world,
and not after Christ.

- Lying

- Fantasies

- Delusions

- Rationalizing

- Wrong Doctrine

- Misuse of Scripture

FEAR

Matthew 25:25-27 NIV So I was afraid and went out and hid your gold in the ground. See, here is what belongs to you.' "His master replied, 'You wicked, lazy servant! So you knew that I harvest where I have not sown and gather where I have not scattered seed? Well then, you should have put my money on deposit with the bankers, so that when I returned I would have received it back with interest.

- Compulsions

- Phobias

- Perfectionism

- Failure

- Inability to set goals

- Laziness

The unsuspecting believer is unaware of the spiritual frauds, working to gain ground inside their minds against them. A stronghold supports its strength by entrenching itself deeply into a person's psyche or perspective, partnering with our carnal natures, which already have a mind that is enmity with God. The "carnal mind" alone shows a natural resistance to God's word in how an unregenerated person may behave or speak.

When coupled with a lie planted by the enemy, "instinctual resistance" to God's word

The "carnal mind" alone shows a natural resistance to God's word in how an unregenerated person may behave or speak.

becomes "active resistance" to God's word. As long as that stronghold remains, a person can be preached to, counseled, and pleaded with to no avail. They can only see matters through their lens of perspective.

We must allow the same mind in Christ to also be in us (Philippians 2:5). If we desire to strive for His standard of living, we must seek his measure of humility and service. As I once preached, "Lose Your Mind," we must be willing to do so to grow in God's wisdom. The carnal mind is at war with God. Strongholds lay the foundation of their fortress in the bedrock of our carnal thinking. These weeds Jesus describes in Mark 4:18-20 represent the "cares of this life" that choke the word of God, making it unfruitful in our lives. Strongholds intend to prevent the word of God from taking root. That is why we are instructed to put on the mind of Christ in 1 Corinthians 2:16.

In Matthew 12:43-45 NLT, Jesus says, *"When an evil spirit leaves a person, it goes into the desert, seeking rest but finding none. Then it says, 'I will return to the person I came from.' So it returns and finds its former home empty, swept, and in order. Then the spirit finds seven other spirits more evil than itself, and they all enter the person and live there. And so that person is worse off than before. That will be the experience of this evil generation."* You may have noticed during this chapter that we've periodically paused to survey various groupings of strongholds, their behavioral fruits, and tendencies.

Jesus reveals to us in Matthew 12:43-45 that our

Lives that are swept clean by the gospel have to be kept clean by the gospel.

spiritual battles are not only a matter of getting free but staying free. Once a truth is learned, an evil spirit is cast out, or a measure of deliverance is gained, a person will experience a season of freedom. That season, however, will do us little good if we only rejoice over being free instead of working to be filled. Lives that are swept clean by the gospel have to be kept clean by the gospel. The enemy will try us again; he will not come alone the next time he comes.

When dealing with the sins and inequities familiar to you, do not allow yourself to be deceived by the enemy's flattery of "spiritual maturity." Knowing what it took for you to break free from its grasp, it returns with reinforcements to reclaim you as its house. Why should we be so casual with the sins that once defeated us and know us best? If any spirit knows our heart and its weak spots, it would be the "squatter" that has dwelled with us the longest. Often, when Jesus healed or forgave a person, he would encourage them, saying, "Go and sin no more." His expectation wasn't that they would live a perfect life, but that they would live circumspectly, never to commit "the sin" that so easily entangled them in the first place, as Hebrews 12: 1 describes. If we fall again to what was once familiar to us, we will eventually find ourselves entertaining strange things. After healing the lame man at the pool of Bethesda in John 5, Jesus explicitly warns him in verse

14 by saying, *"Now you are well; so stop sinning, or something even worse may happen to you."*

Another reason for our vigilance is that stronghold groupings typically happen over time. The enemy has centuries of temptation experience and knows how to leverage the momentum of occasional compromise to his advantage. My mother would say, "Boy, if you will lie, then you will steal!" Being young, hearing this for the first time, perhaps being caught in a "little lie" myself, sounds like an extreme overreaction. In my young mind, I would think, "How could you say that? I would never steal from you, Mom! That's an unfair thing to say." In her mind, she knows her son is not a liar or a thief, but if she lets me get away with this lie, I will become a thief eventually, if not immediately. Lives that are swept clean by the gospel have to be kept clean by the gospel.

The blind spots produced by strongholds can be devastating for the person unaware of the problems they cause by not connecting the dots revealed to them by life experiences. The person affected by strongholds views their approach and responses to life as entirely logical. In emotionally charged situations, their vision becomes clouded as they consider themselves wholly justified in feeling the way they do and, in many cases, biblical. Engaging in spiritual warfare while being led by our carnal inclinations is impossible. As Paul once said about some Creten believers, "They profess that they know God; but in works they deny him, being abominable, and disobedient, and unto every good work reprobate" (Titus 1:16 KJV). When people lose their conscience and moral or spiritual sensitivity to an issue, they cannot agree with what God says regarding that particular truth. Take a look at this last batch of groupings. Though they may not initially appear as provocative as the ones previously explored, they are in many ways the most insidious, for they affect the heart in ways that allow people to keep their religious practices while remaining in the enemy's prison.

BITTERNESS

> **Hebrews 12:15** See to it that no one comes short of the grace of God; that no root of bitterness springing up causes trouble, and by it many be defiled;

- Resentment

- Hate

- Unforgiveness

- Anger

- Violence

- Revenge

HEAVINESS

Psalm 69:20 Reproach hath broken my heart; and I am full of heaviness: and I looked for some to take pity, but there was none; and for comforters, but I found none.

- Depression

- Despair

- Self-Pity

- Loneliness

- Addictions

- Suicide

INSECURITY

Matthew 6:31-32 Therefore take no thought, saying, What shall we eat? or, What shall we drink? or, Wherewithal shall we be clothed? (For after all these things do the Gentiles seek:) for your heavenly Father knoweth that ye have need of all these things.

- Inferiority

- Inadequacy

- Timidity

- Shyness/Withdrawal

- Pleasing people, not God

- Lack of trust/worry

- Wrong relationships

- Quick-tempered

CONTROL

Esther 3:5-6 When Haman saw that Mordecai would not kneel down or pay him honor, he was enraged. Yet having learned who Mordecai's people were, he scorned the idea of killing only Mordecai. Instead Haman looked for a way to destroy all Mordecai's people, the Jews, throughout the whole kingdom of Xerxes.

- Manipulation

- Striving

- Lack of Trust

- Worry

- Insensitivity

- Desire for Recognition

JEALOUSY

James 3:16 For where envying and strife is, there is confusion and every evil work.

- Spitefulness

- Gossip/slander

- Betrayal

- Critical spirit

- Judgmental

- Suspicious nature

IDOLATRY

Isaiah 44:9-10 They that make a graven image are all of them vanity; and their delectable things shall not profit; and they are their own witnesses; they see not, nor know; that they may

be ashamed. Who hath formed a god, or molten
a graven image that is profitable for nothing?

- Frustration

- Hopelessness

- Selfishness/Greed

- Financial problems

- Wrong goals/Decisions

- Confusion/Living a lie

- Pursuing dead ends

- Spiritual blindness/Apathy

- Distractions

Remember, this is only a partial list illuminating the broader
implications of stronghold activity. Stronghold is not an evil
word; it's a military word. Setting up stronghold positions
for any army is essential for gaining ground, keeping ground,
and protecting what's valuable. As believers, we must come
out of and tear down the enemy's strongholds by constantly
renewing our minds and fortifying ourselves within God's

stronghold. May the Lord continue to uphold all of us in Jesus' name.

> Proverbs 18:10 NKJV proclaims, ***The name of the Lord is a strong tower [stronghold]; The righteous run to it and are safe.*** (emphasizes added)

Glossary

That we are not ignorant of his devices...

Spirit of Divination (Python)

Acts 16:16, Jeremiah 14:14, Ezekiel 13:7

This is the practice of attempting to foretell future events or discover hidden knowledge by occult or supernatural means Manifestations – fortunetellers-Soothsayers, Warlocks-Satanist- witches, Rebellion, Drugs

Familiar Spirit

Isaiah 8:19, Acts 8:9,1 Chronicles 10:13

A spirit or demon that serves or prompts an individual, specifically in cases of hidden knowledge, ancestral connections, or a medium that seeks the dead for information. A familiar spirit can also be seducing, making one believe they can be trusted and believed.

Manifestations – Yoga, Drugs, Passive Mind Dreamers, False Prophecy

Religious Spirit

Mark 7:10-13, Matthew 23:27-28, Matthew 23:15-16, Isaiah 1:11-15, Amos 5:21-23, Isaiah 29:13, Ezekiel 33:31, 2 Timothy 3:5

A zealous spirit with a desire to be seen as right rather than repenting as God demands. A person influenced by this spirit spends a great deal of time learning while little time is spent practicing what they profess unless there is an audience around to appreciate their actions. Much attention is given to title, rank, and status, not as a means to give honor but as a way of demonstrating self-value.

Manifestations – Self Righteousness, critical, judgemental, unforgiveness, envy, presumptuous, ungiving, talkative, superficial, fear of people, easily offended

Spirit of Jealousy

Ephesians 5:3, Colossians 3:5, Proverbs 27:4, 1 Timothy 6:4, Job 5:2, Proverbs 14:30, Titus 3:3

Strong emotions of resentment against a person enjoying success or advantage, etc.,

Manifestations –Murder, Revenge-Spite, Anger-Rage, Jealousy, Hatred, Cruelty, Strife, Contention, Competition, Envy, Cause Divisions

Lying Spirit

Proverbs 26:28, Jonah 2:8, Proverbs 6:17, Proverbs 21:6, Proverbs 10:18, 1 Kings 22:23, 2 Thessalonians 2:10-12, Romans 1:25

lying is not a thing but a personality. One becomes possessed with lying to which they become a host.
Manifestations – Strong Deceptions, Flattery, Superstitions, Religious Bondages, False Prophecy, Accusations, Slander, Gossip, Lies, False Teachers

Perverse Spirit

2 Peter 2:1-3, Acts 20:30, 1 Timothy 6:5, Isaiah 19:14,

This is a drawing and alluring spirit. It pulls you in a negative direction. The power and force behind this spirit is strong.
Manifestations – Broken Spirit, Evil Actions, Atheist, Abortion, Child Abuse, Filthy Mind, Sex Perversions, Twisting The Word, Foolish, Chronic Worrier, Contentions, Incest, Pornography

Spirit of Haughtiness

Proverbs 21:24, Ezekiel 16:50, Isaiah 3:16, 2 Timothy 3:2, 1 Timothy 6:4, Proverbs 16:5,

It gives one a big attitude to make them feel like they are better than others and makes you look down on others.
Manifestations – Arrogant-Smug, Pride, Idleness, Scornful, Strife, Self-Deception, Contentious, Self-Righteous, Rebellion, Rejection of God

Spirit of Heaviness

Psalm 32:4, Ezra 9:5, Psalm 69:20, Proverbs 18:14

This comes when the foundation of self-esteem has been badly shaken. It weighs on the mind.
Manifestations – Excessive Mourning, Sorrow-Grief, Insomnia, Self-Pity, Rejection, Broken-Heart, Despair-Dejection-Hopelessness, Depression, Suicidal Thoughts, Inner Hurts-Torn Spirit

Spirit of Whoredom

Hosea 4:11, Leviticus 19:29, 2 Timothy 3:3, 1 Corinthians 10:6, 2 Peter 2:10, 1 Corinthians 6:16, Ezekiel 23:19

Naturally, this spirit is one that has no faithfulness to abstain from the flesh and has no heart for the pain it causes to others to please their lust. It means the same spiritually as one who has cheated on God placing everything over God.

Manifestations – Unfaithfulness/Adultery, Spirit-Soul-or-Body Prostitution, Chronic Dissatisfaction, Love of Money, Fornication, Idolatry, Excessive Appetite, Worldliness

Spirit of Infirmity

Luke 13:11, Romans 6:19, 2 Chronicles 21:19, Matthew 4:23, Deuteronomy 7:15

Manifestations – Bent Body-Spine, Impotent-Frail-Lame, Asthma-Hay Fever-Allergies, Arthritis, Weakness, Lingering Disorders, Oppression, Cancer, Deaf and Mute

Deaf and Dumb Spirit

Mark 9:25, Matthew 12:22, Luke 11:14 (spiritually dull of understanding Hebrews 5:11-13), Matthew 13:13-15, Acts 28:27, Ezekiel 12:2

Manifestations – Dumb-Mute, Crying, Drown, Tearing, Blindness, Mental Illness, Ear Problems, Suicidal, Foaming At The Mouth, Seizures/Epilepsy, Burn, Gnashing Of Teeth

Spirit of Bondage

John 8:34, Romans 7:8, Romans 6:6, 1 Corinthians 15:56

Manifestations – Fears, Addictions (Drugs, Alcohol, Cigarettes, Food, Etcetera…), Fear of Death, Captivity to Satan, Servant of Corruption, Compulsive Sin, Bondage to Sin

Spirit of Fear

1 John 4:18, Proverbs 3:25, Matthew 10:28, Job 4:11-15, Proverbs 29:25, Jeremiah 48:44

Manifestations - Fears-Phobias, Heart Attacks, Torment-Horror, Fear of Man, Nightmares-Terrors, Anxiety-Stress, Fear of Death, Untrusting

Seducing Spirits

1 Timothy 4:1, Mark 13:22, Revelation 2:20, 2 Peter 2:14, Proverbs 14:25

Manifestations –Hypocritical Lies, Seared Conscience, Attractions, Fascinations by false prophets, signs and wonders,

Deception, Wandering from the Truth, Fascination with evil ways objects or persons, Seducers-Enticers

Spirit of Anti-Christ

1 John 2:18, 1 John 2:22, 1 John 4:3, 2 John 1:7, John 17:12, 2 Thessalonians 2:3

Manifestations – Denies Deity of Christ, Denies Atonement, Against Christ and His Teaching, Humanism, Worldly Speech and Actions, Teachers of Heresies, Anti-Christian, Deceiver, Lawlessness

Spirit of Error

2 Peter 3:17, Jude 1:11, 2 Peter 2:18, Isaiah 32:6, 1 John 4:6, 1 Timothy 1:5-7

Manifestations – Error, Unsubmissive, False Doctrines, Unteachable, Servant of Corruption, Contentions, Defensive/Argumentative (defend "Gods revelations" to them personally

Spirit of Poverty

Proverbs 28:22, Proverbs 24:33-34, Proverbs 6:10-11, Proverbs 11:24, Proverbs 23:21

A spirit of poverty has nothing to do with how much anyone owns what they eat or wear. A spirit of poverty can oppress, and not infrequently do, wealthy people. Many people below the "poverty level" are not oppressed by this spirit. It has nothing to do with wealth or lack of it. It is related to greed and fear of loss. A spirit of poverty can be defined as a demonic spirit empowered by iniquity and sin in the areas of giving and receiving. It operates generationally through iniquity. Therefore, it is a familiar (or family-line) spirit. This spirit is related to Belial, the destroyer, described in Psalm 18:4 and 2 Corinthians 6:15. A spirit of poverty is a condition in a person, a people, and/or a land.

Manifestations: Laziness, Greed, Looting, Stealing, Concealing Sin, Lack of Generosity

Spirit of Death

1 John 3:14, Romans 5:12, Job 38:17, Philippians 2:8, Revelation 20:14, Revelation 9:6, Job 24:17, Mark 5:5

Manifestations – Suicide attempts, Despair, Self-mutilation, Recklessness

Bp. Donnell Long

Sr. Pastor, Scripture Cathedral Ministries

Bishop Clarence D. Long is the Senior Pastor of Scripture Cathedral Ministries. Bishop Long was ordained to this high office on Saturday, October 9, 2021. Bishop Long has been ministering the Gospel of Jesus Christ for over two decades. He has embraced his Pastorate and the Bishopric, fiercely determined to lead God's people according to His statutes and precepts.

Bishop Long comes from a long line of service in the Apostolic church. He served under his father's (Apostle C.L. Long) influential leadership and, in doing so, humbled himself to make his confession of devoted service and life-long dedication to God at an early age. In 1988, Bishop Long was ordained as a minister to preach and teach the gospel of Jesus Christ with fervency.

March 31, 2015, would be a somber yet monumental occasion, as the celebratory eulogistic service was held as Pastor Long laid to rest his father, the late Apostle C. L. Long. Yet in that same service through the laying on of hands by Bishop Ralph Dennis and Arch Bishop Alfred A. Owens, (then) Elder Long was consecrated as Pastor and Successor of the Scripture Cathedral Ministries, Inc.

Pastor Long is the loving and proud husband of his wife, Elder Doretha T. Long. They have been wed in holy matrimony since 1988 and have one daughter, Promise Tinsley Long. He and his family have vowed to serve God and his people as they lead the flock of God to that land flowing with Milk and Honey. You are always welcome to worship with us here at the [1] Scripture Cathedral. We are a "Praise 1st Unified Church."

JOIN US

1. www.thescm.church